Acknowledgements

This study was co-ordinated by the NCH Action For Children Policy Unit. Tracey Higgins developed the questionnaire and interview schedules, supervised the fieldwork and analysed the qualitative data. The interviews were carried out by Tracey Higgins, Kit Ward and Cathy Adams. Dr. Tim Lobstein analysed the quantitative data. The report was written by Caroline Abrahams.

NCH Action For Children would like to thank the staff working at its family centres across Britain who were so helpful in carrying out the research. Jeanette Forman helped with the design of the questionnaire. Thanks are also due to Mike Munnelly, NCH Action For Children child protection adviser, and Helen Dent, Director of Policy and Information at NCH Action For Children, for their help in framing this report, its conclusions and recommendations.

But above all, we would like to thank the mothers and children who took part in this research - some of whom had never spoken to anyone before about their personal experiences of domestic violence. We hope that this report does justice to their views.

Please note: domestic violence is a distressing subject, particularly when children are involved. This report contains some explicit descriptions by women and children of the violence they have experienced, and may therefore be unsuitable reading for children and very young people.

Contents

on children who had also been abused by the violent partner and on 'child witnesses' of domestic violence, compared; growing up away from their mothers; disrupted education; leaving home; discussion.

Summary of key findings

During Spring 1994 anonymous questionnaires aimed at mothers who had suffered domestic violence were placed in NCH Action For Children's family centres across Britain. Three weeks later, 108 women, who had 246 children living with them, had returned completed questionnaires. This formed the sample for the survey part of the study.

NCH Action For Children family centres are community-based resources which aim to work with children in need and at risk and their families, not specifically with women and children suffering from domestic violence.

Following the survey, in-depth interviews were carried out with 15 mothers and with 7 children who had also experienced domestic violence.

1. Children's experiences of violence

- Almost three quarters of the mothers in the survey said their children had witnessed violent incidents, and almost two thirds of children had seen their mothers beaten by their violent partners.
- A quarter of the mothers said their violent partners had also physically assaulted their children. Several said their partners had sexually abused their children.
- One in ten of the mothers had been sexually abused in front of their children.
- All the mothers said their children had seen them crying and upset because of the violence.

2. What 'living in a violent situation' really means for children and their mothers

- Two thirds of mothers in the survey said they were slapped or punched, and almost half said they were kicked. These assaults were recurrent.
- Four fifths of women in the survey had suffered from black eyes or bruising and almost a quarter from broken bones. Two fifths of the women had been to hospital for treatment for their injuries and one in eight had been admitted for at least an overnight stay.
- Three quarters of women said their partners had withheld money from them, and more than two thirds said they had been prevented from leaving home or had been stopped from talking to other people. Sometimes this controlling behaviour extended to the children.

- More than four fifths of violent men in the study were fathers to one or more children in the affected families.
- The average length of violent relationships of women in the study was 7.3 years.
- There was no evidence in the study to support the theory that drink and drugs "cause" domestic violence, or to suggest that the violence was due to relationships being in terminal decline.
- The violence women in the study experienced was often serious and recurrent and helped to generate a permanent atmosphere of intimidation affecting both mothers and children. Men's violence and abuse quite often seemed to be systematic, sustained and intrinsic to their relationship with other members of the family.

3. The short term effects of domestic violence on children

- Nine in ten of the mothers thought their children had been affected by the domestic violence in the short term.
- Three quarters of mothers said their children had been frightened, half thought their children had become withdrawn and a third said their children had developed bed-wetting problems. More than one in ten of the mothers said their children had responded by running away from home.
- Almost a third of mothers said their children had intervened to try to protect them from the violence, and more than a quarter said their children had tried to protect their brothers and sisters.
- A quarter of mothers said their children had become aggressive towards them, and a third said their children had been aggressive towards other children or had developed problems at school.
- The domestic violence had impacted in the short term on children who had only witnessed it, as well as on those who had themselves been physically assaulted.
- Most children were very confused by the violence and reacted in apparently conflicting ways, reflecting their emotional turmoil.

4. The longer term effects of domestic violence on children

- More than five in six of the mothers thought their children had been affected by the violence in the longer term.
- A third of mothers thought their children had become violent, aggressive and harder to control. Almost a third thought their children had become resentful and embittered, and a fifth thought their children lacked respect for them.
- Almost a third of mothers thought their children lacked self-esteem in the longer term as a result of the domestic violence. A quarter

thought their children had developed problems in trusting people and in forming relationships.

- The domestic violence had impacted in the longer term on children who had only witnessed it, as well as on those who had themselves been physically assaulted.
- More than one in eight of the mothers in the survey had other children who were not living with them as a direct result of the violence. Some of these children were living with their fathers or with other relatives, while others were in residential or foster care.
- The study showed that children's education can be severely disrupted by domestic violence, and that some young people leave home prematurely in an unplanned way to escape it. In this way, the violence damages children's longer term life chances.

5. The impact of domestic violence on women as mothers

- More than three quarters of mothers had found their children harder to look after while they were living in a violent situation because they were so depressed, and more than half thought this was because they were frightened or exhausted.
- In the longer term the study shows that domestic violence can divide mothers from their children because mothers often feel guilty and children feel resentful, and fail to understand why the violence happens. The emotional distance that develops may be made worse because most mothers find it very difficult to discuss the violence with their children.

6. Leaving a violent partner

- Three quarters of mothers in the survey were no longer living in the violent relationship.
- Almost three quarters of the mothers said that they had been deterred from leaving by the hope that their violent partner would change, and almost three quarters had been afraid of reprisals if they left. More than a half were reluctant to leave their home, and half said they had nowhere to go.
- More than half the mothers had stayed for the sake of their children.
- Almost nine in ten mothers said they left when they realised that their violent partner would never change, and more than two thirds said their decision to leave had been prompted by fear that their violent partner would kill them.
- Two thirds of mothers had left for good out of concern for the effect of the violence on their children. Half the mothers left because they were worried that if they stayed their children would be taken into care, and almost a quarter left when their partner began to hit the children.

- When they left, more than nine in ten of the mothers took the children with them.
- More than half the mothers went to stay with relatives when they left their violent partner; a third went to stay with friends, and a third went to a women's refuge.
- After they left, more than three quarters of mothers had to find new friends, and almost two thirds had to register with a new GP. The children of more than two thirds had to make new friends, and almost half had to change schools.

7. How domestic violence can become a shared family secret

- Two thirds of mothers said they couldn't tell anyone about the violence when it first happened. The average time taken to tell someone was between one and two years.
- More than two thirds of the mothers had found it hard to tell professionals about the problems their children might be having because of the violence at home. More than four fifths said this was because they felt guilty, and three quarters said they were afraid their children would be taken away.

8. The help mothers and children want and need

- More mothers found the police, social services and their doctors helpful than unhelpful, but many were frustrated by the style and timing of their interventions.
- Conversely, the statutory services often wanted to help but felt hampered by mothers' apparent unwillingness to leave violent situations and by legal and other constraints.
- More than half the mothers thought their children could have been helped more to deal with the violence at home. Almost three quarters of these women would have liked their children to have received couselling. Almost two thirds thought they should have learned about domestic violence at school, and more than two fifths thought their children would have benefitted from having somewhere safe to go.

Introduction

NCH Action For Children commissioned this research in 1994 - for two reasons a particularly appropriate year for this study to be carried out.

Firstly, 1994 is the International Year of the Family, and a number of events have taken place around the world aimed at sharing ideas about how the family unit can be best supported. But in order to do this it is necessary to understand what really happens in families and to acknowledge some of the problems, as well as the many benefits, which family life can bring.

More than anything else, the family should be a means of enabling children to grow into adulthood in a happy, loving and supported environment. The family should give children an understanding of their rights and responsibilities as members of a wider community. NCH Action For Children therefore makes no apology for undertaking this research during this particular twelve month period, nor for drawing attention to the impact on children when family life falls particularly short of the ideal.

Secondly, 1994 is the 125th anniversary of the foundation of NCH Action For Children. When the charity came into existence in 1869, one of the main motivations of its founder, the Reverend Thomas Stephenson, was to safeguard the welfare of the many children living on the streets of central London. Some of those children were homeless because of the destitution of their parents, but it is clear from social historians and novelists such as Dickens that many others had left home because of family violence. Recent research on youth homelessness suggests that unfortunately this often remains true today.

NCH Action For Children's decision to carry out a study into the impact of domestic violence on children was made partly at the suggestion of workers in some of our family centres. These projects do not work specifically with women and children suffering from domestic violence. However, staff reported that domestic violence featured in the lives of many of the mothers and children using the centres – even if it was not usually the reason for their original referral, or indeed openly acknowledged by them. Particular concern was expressed about the impact of violence at home on children and about the difficult practice issues that could sometimes arise for staff seeking to work with the mother and the child.

The notion that domestic violence's impact on children is often both severe and underestimated was reinforced by some of the staff in NCH Action For Children's projects which work with homeless young people.

They reported that, in their experience, domestic violence between the adults at home was quite frequently the cause of young people leaving home prematurely and becoming homeless.

This professional experience led to the development of a wider view within NCH Action For Children that as a society we were in danger of failing to recognise the importance of the impact of domestic violence on children. As a result society is probably failing to provide sufficient help and support for the children, young people and mothers concerned. This research seeks to address our lack of knowledge about the impact of domestic violence on children and to increase our understanding of the help children and their mothers need to overcome the trauma and emotional distress which the violence causes.

The impact of domestic violence on children: the research background and policy context

i) The research background

Note: This section is intended to provide only a basic context to the study findings. Much of the information presented here is drawn from two literature reviews: one British, carried out by Lorna Smith, and one Canadian, by Fantuzzo and Linqduist. (References for both will be found in the footnotes). Readers who wish to know more are especially advised to consult these papers.

The nature and prevalence of domestic violence

It is estimated that between 90% and 97% of all domestic violence is directed towards women, by men, largely because of the unequal position of women in society [1]. There is a clear consensus of view that domestic violence occurs in all societies, irrespective of class, race, culture and religion [2].

It is also known that, at least in Western societies, domestic violence is often a hidden problem because it generally occurs in the home and because many women are too ashamed or too frightened to seek help.

This makes it extremely difficult to estimate the prevalence of domestic violence within relationships. In 1975, the Select Committee on Violence in Marriage5 said: "despite our efforts we are unable to give any estimates on what the likely numbers are." Fourteen years later, similar conclusions were reached by Lorna Smith [3].

However, domestic violence forms the second most common type of violent crime reported to the police in Britain, comprising more than 25% of all reported violent crime [4]. In London alone there were 9,800 domestic violence assaults recorded in 1992 [5]. It has been suggested that as few as 2% of such offences are ever reported to the police [6], although opinion differs widely on this issue. The British Crime Survey (1992) estimates that there are 530,000 assaults on women by men in the home each year and in 90% of cases children are in the same or an adjacent room.

There is a consensus of view that the increase in reported domestic violence crimes over recent years in Britain is at least partly explained by improvements in police practice which have encouraged more women to come forward. Certainly, the rise in this type of reported crime is startling. In London, for example, the number of reported domestic violence assaults increased more than twelvefold between 1985 and 1992 [7].

It has also been estimated that one in a hundred marriages are characterised by severe and repeated physical violence [8], and another study has found that 7% of relationships may be violent at some point [9]. A representative national U.S. sample of over 1000 women, and a survey of over 1000 women in the state of Kentucky, found that 20-30% of women reported that physical violence occurred at some time in their marriage. The studies also found that repeated physical abuse took place in about 10% of couples, this being more common among those aged 20-30 [10].

Explanations of domestic violence

Explanations of domestic violence resolve into theories around:

i) Individual pathology. This approach treats domestic violence as exceptional behaviour and places the responsibility for solutions entirely on the individuals concerned. The idea, popularised by Erin Pizzey, that some women are positively attracted to violent relationships gained a great deal of publicity in the early 1980s and was [11]. However, more recent research has failed to find evidence to support this view [12].

ii) Social structural explanations, in which individual, group, cultural and social factors, interacting in complex ways, are all believed to be important. While individual explanations blame the victim and the abuser, the social structuralist approach holds society largely responsible. The problem with this perspective, however, is that it is unable to explain why violence is seen as an appropriate response by some people and not others.

iii)   Feminist explanations, which view all violence as a reflection of unequal power in the relations between men and women [13]. Some writers assert that domestic violence is best understood as an extreme form of normality, an exaggeration of how men are expected by society to behave. Men carry authority in the family, and the family is a microcosm of society [14].

Some writers view the economic dependency of women as an important factor [15], and arguments between men and women over money have been found by researchers to be quite frequent precursors of violent incidents [16]. Jealousy and conflicting expectations about appropriate behaviour for women have also been found to be the causes of discord and violence between partners [17].

The evidence concerning the influence of alcohol and drugs is mixed. On the whole, though, the research supports the view that most incidents of domestic violence do not involve men who are intoxicated and that even when they do, the abuse of alcohol or drugs has not 'caused' the violence [18].

There is no compelling evidence to support the popular notion of a "cycle of violence" as an explanation of domestic violence. This theory suggests that children who experience or witness violence at home are more likely to become involved in violence as adults. The problem with this idea is that the evidence suggests that some, but by no means all, children who are exposed to violence in this way are more likely to become involved in violence as adults, and that not all violent adults have experienced violence as children. In general, the evidence for the perpetuation of an intergenerational cycle of violence is stronger for boys (as abusers) than for girls (as victims) [19].

Children's experiences of domestic violence

Much less has been written about the subject of domestic violence and children compared to that of domestic violence and women, and most of the published research is North American. However, a British study [20] has found that almost half of domestic violence attacks take place in front of others and that three fifths of the observers were the couple's own children.

A recent, but small scale, American study [21] has examined mothers' views of their children's experiences of, and involvement in, domestic violence. The research was based on interviews with 24 self-selected women, recruited through "shelters" (as refuges are termed in the U.S.). Of the participants 70% reported that their children had witnessed the violence or its after effects, and 55% said that their children were direct witnesses to the emotional and physical abuse they had suffered. of the women, 55% left their violent partner for the children's sake.

The impact of domestic violence on children

There is strong research evidence in support of the notion that children are often deeply affected by exposure to family violence. Two well known American studies [22], for example, are often cited in support of the view that children with backgrounds of family violence have a higher incidence of behaviour problems and generally less developed social skills than other children. These studies and others have also suggested that, overall, boys tend to be affected more profoundly than girls.

Research also supports the view that children in general, and girls in particular, who are exposed to family violence tend to be more anxious and/or more depressed than other children [23]. A study has also found that children exposed to conjugal violence had poor concentration and difficulty with school work [24].

However, Fantuzzo's and Lindquist's 1989 review of all the published American research concerning the impact of domestic violence on children[25] suggests that much of this data is far less conclusive than might perhaps be thought. This is for two reasons. Firstly, researching domestic violence is inherently difficult and sensitive, and it seems that the conclusions of many studies have been weakened by a number of unresolved methodological problems.

These typically include: a failure to define the nature and extent of the violence witnessed or experienced by children; lack of control groups; mothers as the sole reporters of the effects on children; over-reliance on samples of mothers and children drawn from women's refuges; and failure to take account of other possible variables relevant to child and family stress, such as poverty and high unemployment.

Some of the authors of these studies are acutely aware of these problems, not least Wolfe et al , who point out that their study is unable, in particular, to show why some children appear to be affected much more profoundly than others by violence between their parents. They suspect, however, that much of the explanation for this may lie in "positive parental relationships and social supports... (as)...significant mediators of child adjustment in such situations".

A second criticism made of much of the research by Fantuzzo and Lindquist is that it often fails to take into sufficient account the importance of child abuse and neglect. This is perhaps surprising since what evidence there is tends to suggest that child abuse and domestic violence are quite frequently correlated.

Straus et al [27], for example, found that there was a 129% greater chance of child abuse in a home where conjugal violence was present. Similarly, in a study by Bowker et al [28], men who beat their wives also physically abused children in 70% of cases in which children were present at home; and other studies reviewed by Hughes et al[29] reported correlations of 40-60% between child abuse and domestic violence.

Further evidence concerning the impact on children of experiencing domestic violence comes from a rather different source – studies of the characteristics of the population of young homeless people. 'Violence', 'abuse', and 'arguments' are usually the most common reasons young homeless people give for having left home prematurely.

For example, recent research[30] carried out among young homeless people aged between 16 and 25 in Hampshire and Surrey found that 45% of the sample had left home because of arguments, 26% because of violence, and 17% because they were 'asked to leave'.

Youth homelessness studies of this type do not usually detail the nature of the violence which leads to young people leaving home prematurely. However, their findings certainly suggest that 'violence at home' can make life so intolerable for teenagers that the disruption and uncertainty of an unplanned departure – moving between hostels, friends, squats, and the streets – actually offers a better, safer option than staying at home.

ii) The policy context

Domestic violence raises important issues for a number of institutions and professions who come into contact with women and children. This section aims to provide a basic overview of some of these issues.

Central initiatives

In recent years there have been a number of initiatives and reports concerning domestic violence in Britain, the most important of which are: i)a House of Commons Home Affairs Select Committee investigation (and report) into domestic violence (1992); ii)a Law Commission investigation and report concerning the family law, domestic violence and occupation of the family home (1992); iii)a national, inter-agency working party inquiry and report concerning domestic violence, convened by Victim Support (1992), and iv)a ministerial group on domestic violence established by Michael Jack, Minister of State at the Home Office (1993).

In October 1994, the ministerial group on domestic violence endorsed an inter-departmental public awareness campaign on domestic violence - *"Domestic violence - don't stand for it!"*. The campaign consisted of advice leaflets and posters and the re-run of a cinema advert originally made for the Women's Aid Federation in 1993. At the same time, an inter-departmental circular was issued to encourage relevant agencies (eg. the police, social services, housing authorities, voluntary organisations) to develop a co-ordinated, multi-disciplinary response to domestic violence.

Police

"The police are the gatekeepers of the criminal justice system and any discussion of the response of the system must begin by welcoming the growing concern of the police over matters of domestic violence in recent years and the many recent innovations and improvements in their guidelines and practice." (From *Domestic Violence: report of a national inter-agency working party*, Victim Support, 1992.)

In 1987, the Metropolitan Police circulated a Force Order containing the instruction to treat domestic violence incidents as potential criminal offences to all their officers . This marked a significant change in police attitudes.

In 1990, the Home Office issued a helpful Circular (no. 60/1990) extending this approach to all police forces. The circular called on police to implement the criminal law firmly and also to work co-operatively with other agencies in the context of domestic violence. The Circular states: *"It is the immediate duty of police officers who are called to a domestic violence incident to secure the protection of the victim and any children from further abuse and then to consider what action should be taken against the offender."*

Many police forces have now established 'domestic violence units' to provide a readily accessible and sensitive service to women experiencing domestic violence. In London, for example, 62 of the Metropolitan Police's 69 divisions maintain domestic violence units. The establishment of these units probably largely explains the upsurge in the number of domestic violence incidents reported to police (see the research background: the nature and prevalence of domestic violence, above.)

Some police forces have set up initiatives which co-ordinate their services concerning child abuse and domestic violence. West Yorkshire Police, for example, maintain a computerised index which links domestic violence and child abuse on the basis that: *"The more information that is made available to an officer who attends the scene of any domestic incident, the better this enables him to make a more professional, informed decision... if there is a child at risk in the house (the officer) will be encouraged to go out of his/her way to see that the child is both safe and well"*[31]. Similarly, Strathclyde Police operate a 'child and family unit' staffed by specialist officers who work on issues including child abuse, domestic violence and truancy.

However, such joint child abuse/domestic violence initiatives have not always been welcomed for fear that resources tend to be concentrated on the statutory investigation of child abuse to the neglect of domestic violence issues[32].

Refuges

Refuges provide many women and children with somewhere safe to go (as well as providing support to those living with violence), and as such they are a vital resource for women and children wishing to leave violent situations. About two in every three women who use refuges have children, and many refuges include specialist workers in their staff teams to work with children. Some refuges have been established to work specifically with women and children from ethnic minorities.

Each year about 30,000 women and children use refuges in Britain and over 100,000 women contact the Women's Aid Federation (WAFE) for support. However, in 1990, WAFE were only able to find space in their refuges for 40% of the women requesting shelter. In 1975, the Select Committee on Violence in Marriage recommended that there should be 1 family refuge space per 10,000 population, and yet almost twenty years later, Britain is less than a third of the way towards meeting this comparatively modest target.

The Department of Health grant aids WAFE and other umbrella bodies annually to co-ordinate refuge provision. There are 284 refuges in Britain [33], the overwhelming majority of which operate as independent voluntary organisations, relying heavily on local authority funding, topped up with housing benefit from residents, charitable donations and, in the case of refuges working in partnership with housing associations, grant payments from the Housing Corporation. Refuge funding has never been secure or plentiful, but in recent months there has been particular concern that local authority funding cuts are seriously threatening the survival of some refuges.

Housing and the law

A number of important housing and related legal issues arise for women and children in violent situations. At present women are able to apply to the civil courts for injunctions for two specific purposes:

i) a 'non-molestation injunction' to keep a violent partner from attacking them

ii) an 'ouster injunction' to remove a violent partner from their home.

These injunctions are designed to provide temporary solutions and are granted on a time-limited basis, although they may be renewed. A non-molestation injunction is granted much more readily by the courts than an ouster injunction, since English law is very reluctant to interfere with property rights, except in the most serious circumstances.

Enforcing an injunction can be difficult: a power of arrest can be attached to a non-molestation injunction so that the police are empowered to arrest the violent partner if he breaks its terms, but usually only if there is evidence to present to the court of actual bodily harm having already been caused. Without a power of arrest, breach of the injunction may be contempt of court, the remedy for which is to return before the original (civil) court, but this is little comfort to the woman at home whose violent partner is trying to batter down the door. Of nearly 26,000 non-molestation injunctions granted in 1992, only 9,660 had powers of arrest attached.

At present the law relating to injunctions is contained in several different statutes, according to the different situations in which they may come to be used. The Law Commission has recently investigated the civil law relating to domestic violence and occupation of the family home and has recommended a number of changes designed to improve the law and make it more consistent in this area. Three recommendations in the Law Commission report[34] of particular relevance to this study are the following:

i) amendment of the Children Act 1989 to give courts the power to make a short-term emergency ouster order against an abusing parent for the protection of the child

ii) the introduction of a "balance of harm" test when courts are considering the granting of orders regulating occupation of the family home[35]

iii) The adoption of a presumption in favour of attaching powers of arrest to non-molestation injunctions when there has been violence or threatened violence.

In June 1994, the Lord Chancellor announced the Government's intention to implement most of the recommendations contained in the Law Commission report, "when a suitable opportunity occurs".

The need for women and children fleeing violence to be safe in the short term is the immediate concern, but thereafter, if a separation from the violent partner is to be more than merely temporary, the question of securing permanent alternative accommodation arises. Some refuges have limited access to local authority or housing association housing stocks, but the supply is always less than the demand, and, in any event, many women and children who leave violent partners do not use refuges.

Many women and children leaving violent situations are, therefore, dependent on the homelessness safety net, as presently set out in Part Three of the Housing Act 1985, for access to alternative accommodation. In theory, as the law presently stands, a mother with dependent children who is homeless because of violence is in priority need and entitled to be housed. In practice, difficulties sometimes arise.

Most of these problems are related to the fact that local authority housing stocks are usually too small to meet the needs of homeless applicants and others in acute housing need, so various 'rationing measures' are used by authorities. Women and children fleeing violence therefore struggle to gain permanent housing in the same way as other groups of homeless people. This forces many to stay in unsuitable temporary accommodation (including 'bed and breakfast hotels' in some cases) for long periods of time.

Some special problems can also arise for homeless women and children escaping violence, as recent research shows[36]. Firstly, they may need to move to a different area to be safe from the violent partner. According to the legislation, women who have left their home area because of violence should not be asked to prove a local connection with the authority they apply to, but it appears that in some authorities it is very difficult for women and children without a local connection to be rehoused.

Secondly, asking women to provide evidence of violence by seeking legal advice with a view to taking possible legal action against the perpetrator and returning to their original home, is becoming standard practice in many authorities, particularly in London, which are experiencing acute housing crisis. This policy leads to long delays in decision making as well as causing some applications to be refused. Judgements of intentional homelessness are quite commonly made against women because they are unwilling to return home after obtaining an injunction (despite the problems in enforcing court orders, noted above).

Thirdly, women made homeless by domestic violence who are owner-occupiers (usually jointly with the violent perpetrator) may face particular difficulties in applying as homeless to their local authority. They may be considered to be intentionally homeless if they fail to pursue their claim to the family home, or their application may be held up while legal proceedings are completed.

Fourthly, some women who leave home through violence and are unable to secure permanent housing very speedily, if at all, face the loss of their children to their securely housed partners. That children may be returned to the woman's violent partner or separated from their mother purely on accommodation grounds is very disturbing. It is contrary to the spirit of both the homelessness legislation and the emphasis on the interests of children and young people in the Children Act 1989.

Finally, older children may be separated from their mothers in another way. The homelessness legislation bestows a right to housing onto a woman and her 'dependent' children. 'Dependence' is defined in financial terms, and refers to children aged 16 and under. The Guidance to the homelessness legislation suggests that all authorities should normally include: *"All children under 16 and all children aged 16-18 who are in, or are about to begin, full-time education or training, or who for other reasons are unable to support themselves and who live at home."* So, for example, a 17 year old daughter who is working would not fall within the definition and might have to live elsewhere, even if both she and her mother would like to have lived together.

However, if the situation for women and children fleeing violence and seeking rehousing is less than easy under the present law, it threatens to become much more problematic in the near future. For in January 1994 the Government issued a Green Paper, *"Access to local authority and housing association tenancies"*, which proposed the repeal of the present homelessness legislation.

A feature of the proposed new scheme which will be particularly damaging to women and children leaving violent situations is that local authorities will no longer be under a duty to provide permanent accommodation to homeless applicants who meet all the eligibility criteria. Instead, they will be able to discharge their duty to them by arranging for the provision of temporary accommodation for a minimum period of a year, and that accommodation may be in the private sector. This will make it much harder for these women and children (like all other homeless people) to resettle and may act as a further disincentive to leaving for women thinking of escaping a violent situation.

Issues for social workers

On the whole, there is little statutory social work intervention in domestic violence cases. The major exception to this is when a social services department becomes concerned that a child living in a violent situation is at risk of 'significant harm'. In these circumstances the department is under a statutory duty (under the Children Act 1989 in England and Wales) to initiate child protection procedures. In some cases this may result in a case conference involving all the relevant professionals.

A decision may be taken to place the child's name on the authority's child protection register and to devise a child protection plan in partnership with the child's parents. Ultimately, if social services cannot be sure that the child is safe at home, a decision may be taken to remove her or him.

Previous research (see above) shows that domestic violence to a mother and abuse of a child in the family are quite often correlated, so clearly it is important that social workers – as well as other professionals such as police officers – are aware of this potential relationship. However, it seems that this is not always so.

An example of this lack of awareness and the tragic results which can ensue is the death of Sukina Hammond, a five year old girl who was killed by her father in 1988. The investigation into her death [37] found that the failure of the social services department to take sufficient note of Sukina's father's severe violence towards her mother led them seriously to underestimate the threat which he posed to Sukina.

In reflecting on why this happened, the authors of the investigation report wrote: (Paragraph 160) *"The caring professions, on the whole, find it very difficult to differentiate between families under stress, where there is occasional violence, and those where there is a culture of violence. This in part is because the literature on child abuse on the whole ignores this phenomenon and yet literature on criminology deals with the subject in relation to adults in considerable detail. This is particularly significant in this case and is so in other cases. Unless we begin to understand these issues our ability to protect children will be seriously impaired."*

(Paragraph 162) *"It is therefore necessary for those involved in child protection cases to begin to understand that families (where there is a culture of violence) have a lifestyle and behaviour patterns which include the use of systematic violence....The father did not set out to kill Sukina but to impose his will. When he failed to do so the violence escalated until the child died. Because he could not impose his will the father could not stop beating her."*

There is other evidence to support the notion that social work tends to overlook domestic violence and often fails to appreciate its impact on women and children. Children living in refuges are not usually deemed by local authorities to be "children in need" under section 17, Children Act 1989, the provision which triggers entitlement to a range of support services. Similarly, domestic violence does not usually feature on the agendas of Area Child Protection Committees (ACPCs), the bodies which exist to co-ordinate and supervise multi-agency child protection work.

In addition, as WAFE have pointed out[38]: *"The Children Act makes no mention of domestic violence. It assumes that parents are reasonable, loving and caring individuals, both to their children and to each other, even at the point of separation or divorce. It also assumes that where parents do separate, the children will almost always benefit from having continued, frequent and substantial contact with their father."*

Whilst the assumption that parents are invariably reasonable is usually quite fair, it can lead to serious difficulties when, for example, negotiating and carrying out arrangements for residence and contact (access) after a mother has separated from her violent partner. In such situations there is a risk that the child may become a victim and be used as a tool by the violent man to manipulate his ex-partner.

Meetings between separated parents to discuss future arrangements for the children are generally a good idea but probably inappropriate where there has been domestic violence, as the Association of Chief Officers of Probation (ACOP) and the Family Division of the High Court have recognised[39]. However, the Children's Legal Centre's experience, for example, is that court welfare officers sometimes fail to make it clear to women that they have a choice about attending such meetings, and, indeed, that they may impose on them considerable pressure to come[40].

It is also clear that where there has been domestic violence in a family, the court should take particular care to ascertain the wishes and feelings of the child (as they are obliged to do under the Children Act 1989) when considering issues of residence and contact. In the view of some groups, including WAFE and the Children's Legal Centre, courts sometimes fail to do this.

Research Methodology

For the reasons already set out in the Introduction, it was decided to carry out research concerning the impact of domestic violence on children and their mothers during Spring 1994[41] and to base the study mainly[42] on the experiences of mothers and children using NCH Action For Children's family centres.

Family centres are community based projects, designed to provide a range of support services for children who are at risk or in need and their families. These services often include child care facilities, counselling, various support groups and help and advice with benefits and housing. Some centres also provide more formal social work services, including assessments of children who are the focus of legal (civil) proceedings. Family centres aim to work with children and all the relevant members of their families (including, in some cases, grandparents and brothers and sisters), but the most typical consumers of family centre services are children and their mothers.

Family centres tend towards three different models. 'Referred' centres work predominantly with families where child abuse and protection is central; 'neighbourhood' centres provide family support services on a self-referred or a drop-in basis; and 'integrated' centres are a combination of both.

Part Three of the Children Act 1989 sets out the duty of local authorities to provide family support services for children 'in need'. The Audit Commission has recently emphasised how important these services – especially family centres – are in preventing family breakdown and has called on authorities to do more in this respect[43].

NCH Action For Children runs more family centres in Britain than any other voluntary agency, usually in partnership with social services. NCH Action For Children family centres are to be found in inner-city, suburban and rural settings. Many are in areas of extreme social and economic disadvantage where there are high rates of unemployment and acute housing need, and where many families are dependent on welfare benefits.

Therefore the sample in this study could not be said to be an accurate representation of the population of mothers across Britain who suffer from domestic violence. It clearly contains a disproportionate number of women on low incomes, living in socially disadvantaged areas. (The survey sample is also probably unrepresentative in that it contains disproportionately few women from ethnic minorities – see below under *Characteristics of the survey sample.*)

However, it is important to note that NCH Action For Children's family centres do not specifically aim to work with children and mothers suffering from domestic violence, so the study sample was not pre-defined as being one of mothers who were living in violent situations. This distinguishes this study from most previous domestic violence research, the samples for which have usually been drawn exclusively from refuges.

It was decided that the study should have two parts: a survey (quantitative) component with mothers and an interview (qualitative) component with mothers and children.

1. The Survey

Firstly, an anonymous written questionnaire was developed aimed at mothers who had experienced domestic violence. This was successfully piloted on twelve mothers.

Just before Easter 1994, ten questionnaires were sent to each of NCH Action For Children's 108 family centres across Britain. The project leader was asked to place them, plus an advertising poster where they would be visible, but where there was enough privacy for women to take one unobtrusively. It was emphasised in the questionnaire and accompanying letter, and on the poster, that the study was completely anonymous.

The closing date for completed questionnaires was set three weeks later, by which time 108 viable questionnaires had been returned. These 108 questionnaires completed by the women, who were thus self-selecting, formed the survey sample. The survey results were then analysed using a computerised database (SPSS).

Characteristics of the survey sample

- The mean age of respondents was 31; exactly half of the women were in their 20s. (Note: this was the age of the mothers when completing the questionnaire, not necessarily that at which they experienced violence as some were commenting on previous experience of domestic violence. For details of the ages of women when violence occurred see the *Findings*).

- The average number of children living with the respondent at the time of completing the questionnaire was 2.58; most women had 2 children living with them.

- The 108 women had 246 children living with them, and their overall

19

average age was 6.7. In virtually all cases these children were the respondents' own biological children; just two women said that they looked after children who were not theirs.

- Of the 108 women, 14 had other children not living with them as a direct result of the domestic violence: the children of 6 of the mothers were being accommodated by the local authority; those of 3 women were living with relatives; and those of 5 women were living with their ex-partner. (Note: these children were therefore additional to the 246 children in the sample.)

- A question asked respondents to state if they felt that they belonged to a particular ethnic group: 83% did not answer; 2% said that they were Afro-Caribbean; 1% said that they were mixed race, 1% Irish and 1% Welsh; and 12% said that they were white British. From these answers it seems likely that the overwhelming majority of women in the survey were of white European origin. Women from ethnic minorities are therefore probably under-represented in this study.

- Of the respondents 66% had experienced violence from one partner and 34% from more than one. The questionnaire asked respondents to refer to their most recent violent relationship.

- Of the respondents 23% were still living in a violent relationship. Of those who had left, 61% had been in the violent relationship for two years or longer and 35% for five years or more.

- The average duration of the violent relationships of mothers in the survey was 7.3 years.

2. The interviews

It had been decided that a small number of in-depth interviews should be carried out with mothers who had experienced domestic violence so as to gain further understanding of some of the results generated by the first part of the research. In the event, fifteen such interviews took place, and, again, these women were recruited through NCH Action For Children family centres. (There was a question in the questionnaire asking whether women would also be prepared to be interviewed on a confidential basis).

The issue of whether or not to seek to interview children and young people who were experiencing, or who had experienced, domestic violence was discussed at some length. The advantage of doing so would be that the child's perspective would clearly greatly add to the value of the study, but there was concern not to "exploit" for research purposes children and young people who might be very vulnerable. This seemed likely to be a special risk in the case of younger children, who might, we feared, be coerced into taking part by their mothers (albeit with the best of intentions).

In the event, it was decided that the interviews with children should proceed. Seven in-depth interviews were carried out with young people with experience of domestic violence - and these indeed proved to be very valuable. Two of the young people were children of mothers who were also interviewed. Particular care was taken in their cases to ensure that they themselves wanted to take part in the research and that their mothers were also happy for them to do so. The researchers worked closely with social workers in the family centres concerned. The other five teenagers interviewed were recruited through NCH Action For Children projects which work with young homeless people. The children and young people interviewed were all girls between eight and seventeen years of age.

Some of the mothers found the interviews quite stressful, not because of any lack of sensitivity on the part of the interviewers but because of the nature of the subject matter. One mother, for example, became very upset when realising for the first time, during the course of her interview, that she had been completely unaware of where her toddler had been during a violent argument with her partner. In this and other cases project staff were able to provide interviewees with immediate reassurance and support – a good reason for arranging for interviews to take place within NCH Action For Children projects.

Semi-structured interview schedules had been developed and piloted, and the interviews were tape recorded with the permission of the interviewees. The resulting tapes were then transcribed and analysed. Copies of the transcripts were sent to all the interviewees to be checked for any errors, and to ensure that the mothers and young people had, with the benefit of hindsight, the opportunity to withdraw any statements they wished excluded.

Findings

Note: 108 valid questionnaires were returned from women who had children at the time that they experienced domestic violence, but not all respondents answered all questions. The percentages given are calculated with reference to the number of responses received to the particular question. Percentages may not add to 100 because of rounding. Quotations in the text are from mothers rather than from children unless otherwise indicated.

1. Violence in the family

When the violence first began

Table 1: Age of mothers when the violence began

Age	%
below 16	7
16 - 20	41
21 - 25	32
26 - 30	12
31 - 35	7
36 - 42	2

(106 responses)

Almost half (48%) of the mothers who responded to this question said that they first experienced violence from their partner when they were aged 20 or younger. Of these women 7% said that they were actually aged below 16 when the violence began. Four fifths (80%) of respondents had first experienced violence when aged 25 or younger.

Many of these violent partnerships, therefore, started when the women were very young.

"I remember the first time he hit me, he was quite sorry, and I was quite shocked, and I forgave him because I was so madly in love with him and I thought, oh well, it was just one of those things and it wouldn't happen again. So I suppose the first time he did it he got away with it, but it just got worse and worse."

Violence in the context of family formation

Table 2: Number and ages of children in the family when the violence began

Number of children	%	Mean ages of children
none	29	-
one	38	1.6
two	21	4.6, 2.1
three	9	5.2, 3.3, 1.4
four	3	9.3, 6.7, 4.0, 3.0.

(101 responses)

More than two thirds (71%) of women had children when the violence began. (Note: those women who were not mothers when the violence began (29%) subsequently had children while they were still living in a violent relationship). The greatest proportion, almost two fifths, had one child, with an average age of 18 months. Overall, the average age of the children of respondents when the violence began was 3 years.

The majority of respondents in this survey were, therefore, not only young women but young mothers when they first experienced violence from their partners. Being young themselves and having one or more small children of their own means that they were vulnerable emotionally. Given the nature of the survey sample, and the fact that these young mothers would not as yet have developed a career, they were also vulnerable materially.

A significant number of the mothers who were interviewed said that the violence had begun around the time of pregnancy or babyhood, and others claimed that it had started once their children had become toddlers. The women often seemed to believe that this was partly because of their partners' jealousy or possessiveness.

"Things were alright until just after my daughter was born. Every time I picked up the baby, he would go mad.... a real complete jealousy, you know, of this child, and, I mean, I just adored her."

"He suddenly got very possessive again when the baby arrived."

"I had my daughter about eighteen months after being married, thinking it will change him....It made him worse....I don't know why it was. I don't know whether maybe men like that feel threatened by babies, or that they are jealous of them."

The violent men were invariably the fathers

Table 3: Relationship of the violent man to the children in the family

Nature of relationship	%
father of child/children	83
step father to child/children	7
not related to the children	6
no children at the time	5

(105 responses)

As Table 3 shows, in more than four fifths (80%) of cases the violent partner was father to one or more children in the family, and was step father in a further 7% of cases.

When this finding is juxtaposed with the consideration that the average duration of violent relationships in this survey was 7.3 years, it becomes clear that this research tends to refute the popular stereotype that men who are violent in families are often involved in only transient relationships with women, unrelated to any children in the household.

2. The nature of the violence experienced by women

Note: Tables reporting the responses of women to questions about the nature, severity and prevalence of the violence they experienced are shown in full in Appendix 1.

Physical attacks

When women were asked to describe the violence they had experienced, the most common characteristics were: being slapped or punched (86%) and being grabbed or shaken (76%). However, 63% of women also reported that they had been strangled, 61% said that they had been kicked, and 61% also said that they had been struck with an object.

"He kicked me in the stomach when I was pregnant by him. I was about eight weeks, and I suffered a threatened miscarriage... I didn't lose (my son), but it was close."

"I remember one time, I thought he was going to strangle me. I did really think that was the end....I was very frightened."

"Mostly he seemed to go for my head, or he used to pull my hair, put his hand round my throat and hold me against the door and sort of breathe right into my face which I used to hate."

"As I walked out of the living room....my husband pulled me by the hair...and punched me in the face, gave me a bleeding nose and punched me a couple of times in the stomach."

Sexual violence

Almost half of the women (46%) said that they had been forced by their violent partner to have sex against their wishes. Almost a quarter (23%) said that they had been 'raped with threats', and almost a fifth (18%) reported that they had been 'raped with violence'. The proportion of women who said that they had been forced by their partner to read or watch pornography was 17%.

"I love my son dearly, I adore him, but he was conceived in rape."

"Well, basically, he raped me, he was abusive and started head butting me and biting me."

"I felt very used, very dirty."

Frequency and severity of the violence

A significant proportion of women in the survey said that they experienced violence from their partner at least several times each month. For example, two thirds (66%) of respondents said that they were slapped or punched, and more than half (55%) that they were grabbed or shaken with this degree of frequency. Amost half of the women (46%) said that they were kicked at least several times a month.

Over four fifths (83%) of the women had experienced bruises or black eyes, and almost a third (31%) said that they were injured in this way at least several times a month while they were living in the violent situation. Half (50%) of the women said that they had been cut, a fifth (21%) at least several times a month; and almost a quarter (23%) had had broken bones. In addition, some respondents reported that they had been scratched, burnt or had teeth broken during assaults.

Two fifths (40%) of the women had been to hospital for treatment for their injuries, and an eighth (12%) had been admitted for at least an overnight stay.

When these findings concerning the severity and the prevalence of assaults are taken together, a picture emerges of a significant proportion of women in the survey experiencing on-going, serious violence.

"Every week I had one or two black eyes. guaranteed."

"He grabbed hold of my fingers and tried breaking two... I felt like they'd broke... he was just on top of me... kicking me in the face, pulling my hair.... my hair bled at the roots... and I thought my teeth had gone at one stage... .I went to go out the front door and just got there.... he pushed me through the glass of the front door. I was admitted to hospital, and afterwards when I used to sneeze or cough, it used to send shooting pains down through my teeth."

Being insulted and humiliated

Three quarters (75%) of women in the survey said that they had been insulted by their violent partner and called 'stupid' or 'useless' – nearly two thirds of them (61%) at least several times a month. Almost three quarters of respondents had been humiliated by their partner in front of their children (72%) or in front of other people (69%). More than half of the women (52%) said that this happened to them at least several times a month.

"He would just tell them (the children) that I was no good... they'd just stay silent."

"My son was seven weeks old at the time... it was, 'you stupid cow. You're a silly bitch, and you know you're no good to be a mother. You're no good as a wife, and what the hell am I doing here with you?'"

"I would be called a 'Jesus God's whore'.... it was blasphemy and swearing and names".

Men's insults can be very destructive, particularly if they are uttered in front of children or other people so that women feel publicly humiliated. It is important to understand how distressing and undermining this type of behaviour is for women, especially if it is systematic and continues over a long period of time.

The abuse of power through controlling behaviour

A large proportion of respondents gave examples of their violent partners abusing their power over them and seeking to control their behaviour, usually including their freedom of movement. Three quarters (74%) of women, for example, said that their partners had withheld (or taken) money from them, almost two thirds (61%) of them several times a month, at least. More than two thirds (69%) of women had been "not allowed out", more than half (52%) of them more than several times a month; and two thirds (65%) of women had been prevented from speaking to other people, almost half (45%) of them repeatedly.

More than two fifths (44%) of the women said that they had actually been locked in their home by their violent partner to prevent them from leaving, a fifth (19%) of them repeatedly; and more than a fifth (22%) of women had had their clothes taken away, a tenth (10%) of them at least several times a month.

Comments from mothers who were interviewed suggest that in many cases the primary motive behind this type of behaviour was possessiveness and jealousy on the part of the man.

"He stopped any affection between us, myself and the children. He wanted me all to himself. If my children asked me for a cuddle or anything like that, they were asked why."

"(He said) I was a prostitute. I slept with every man I had looked at..."

"I didn't really have any friends because I wasn't allowed to have friends. If I went out with friends... I was being a tart, and I was being a whore."

The desire to prevent other people from knowing that they had injured the women may have motivated some men to keep them at home. At other times the desire to control women's actions seemed to be an end in itself. Some of the women and children who were interviewed made it clear that this "controlling behaviour" also extended to the whole family. (This is further discussed below, under *Children's experiences of violence*).

"We were kept like prisoners, not allowed out - sometimes all weekend. We weren't allowed to see friends or have friends back... he used to physically drag the children back in the house. They were upset that they were not allowed to visit their grandfather who was ill in hospital."

The role of drink and drugs

The survey did not include a question about women's perceptions of the role of drink or drugs in "causing" their partners' violence towards them. However, some of the mothers who were interviewed made reference to drunkenness accompanying the violent behaviour they experienced.

"He had this thing where he wouldn't let her (the daughter) go to bed.... some mornings she never went to bed until 2 or 3am.... I could never understand it, why he would want her to see him behaving badly in that way.... he would make them stay in the same room as him and watch him getting more and more drunk."

None of the mothers who were interviewed said they thought that the violence they had experienced was caused by the intoxication of their violent partner. For some, the violence was so much a feature of their partner's behaviour towards them that no 'external' factor could possibly explain its generation - these men were simply incorrigibly violent:

"He was violent when he was sober as well. Two years before he died, he tried to set fire to me.... He just had a terrible temper.... the slightest thing would set him off."

Moreover, it is clear from the survey findings that in a significant proportion of cases men perpetrated on-going violence and abuse towards their female partners in a systematic way and were fully aware of their actions.

This study, therefore, tends to reinforce previous research findings which show that intoxication due to drink or drugs sometimes, but not always, co-exists alongside domestic violence, but does not in itself cause men's violent behaviour.

Discussion: the realities of 'living in a violent situation'

The women who took part in the survey were asked to differentiate between various types of violent experiences, and their answers are reported thematically above. However, it is important to appreciate that many of them experienced a wide range of these abusive and violent behaviours from their partners, sometimes including violence which was both severe and recurrent.

Almost nine in ten (88%) of the women said that they had also been threatened with violence, more than two thirds (68%) of them repeatedly. It is clear from their reports of the actual violence they had suffered that for the most part these threats were by no means groundless, and as such they would clearly have helped to produce an enduring atmosphere of fear and intimidation.

The cumulative effect of what often appears to be sustained physical and sexual abuse, threats of violence and behaviour designed to undermine and humiliate is what is really meant by the somewhat sanitised expression, 'living in a violent situation'. As many of the women who were interviewed explained, the violence they were suffering frequently took place behind closed doors so that only the children – if anyone – knew what was happening. So far as outsiders were concerned, theirs was often an entirely 'normal' relationship. As one mother commented, *"He was what I called a street angel and a house devil."*

It is abundantly clear, then, from all the evidence reported in this section that the violence that most of the women in the study were experiencing was not the product of relationships in terminal decline in the sense that they were on the verge of complete breakdown. Instead, many of the relationships which were the subject of this research appear as ones in which violence was, or had become, an intrinsic part of how the man behaved towards his female partner, and also (as shown below) his children. In this sense they were, in their own way, 'stable relationships', and, as has already been observed, some had endured for years. For this reason, most of the relationships described in this research are qualitatively different from those in which there is turbulence and discord which is about to lead the partners to decide to separate.

It is probably impossible for those of us who have not experienced domestic violence to understand the impact on women of living in a relationship in which there is sustained, systematic violence. But some of the women gave graphic descriptions of how this made them feel:

"I felt very small all the time. I felt I had to do as I was told because I was afraid if I didn't, I would get a hiding, and I knew that when my husband hit me, it wouldn't just be a slap, it was a proper punch... I was very scared that if my husband did punch me that it wouldn't just be once, it would go on, and it wouldn't stop."

"You just never knew when it was going to come.... I used to end up with maybe two black eyes... and he wouldn't let me out of the house."

"There was an atmosphere in the house the whole time because I was just so afraid of him."

These are relationships in which the men have come to hold all the power, and in which there is no trust or reciprocity. Although the expression 'violent partner' is frequently used in this report, as in others, to describe the male perpetrator of the violence, it is clear that these relationships are not really genuine 'partnerships' in the sense of the terms of the relationship being negotiated.

The depression, shock and sadness which women feel in such circumstances is frequently amplified by the realisation that they are being abused by someone whom they had originally loved and respected. By the time they understand that their partner's behaviour is not going to change, the violence has made them depressed, exhausted and isolated; it has literally disempowered them. It is important to understand this, because this helps to explain why most women find it so extremely hard to leave violent relationships, even though leaving appears to be the 'obvious solution' to domestic violence, so far as outsiders are concerned. (Note: the difficulties which mothers face in leaving a violent relationship are further analysed in a later section).

3. Children's experiences of domestic violence

Almost nine tenths (87%) of respondents said that they believed that their children were aware of the violence at home. Several of the 13 respondents who thought that their children were unaware suggested that this was because their child was only a baby at the time the violence occurred.

Table 4 below illustrates the different ways in which the 87% (86 in number) of mothers thought that their children had become aware of the violence.

Table 4: Children's experiences of domestic violence

nature of children's experiences	%
the children were hit or abused themselves	27
the children witnessed the violence	73
the children overheard one or more attacks	62
the children saw the resulting injuries	52
the children saw their mother upset or crying	99
mothers had discussed the violence with them	17
the children were aware of the violence because of the atmosphere at home/'living in a violent situation'	69

(86 respondents)

Children who were also abused by the violent partner

Table 4 shows that more than a quarter (27%) of the children had been hit or physically abused by the violent man who was usually their father.

"They had to sleep face down, facing the wall... If they moved during the night, they got punched in the back."

"He hit (my son) with a leather belt. He was a very fussy eater...'You bastard, eat that dinner', and he would pick up the belt and just lash him with it. And, of course, I would go for him then, and the next thing, I would get it."

"He used to hit me as well as my Mum... One time he smashed my head against the wall in my bedroom, gave me a black eye, and I had to make excuses at school." (child)

"I never cried, never cried, no matter how hard he hit me... I wouldn't let myself feel it." (child)

One child who was interviewed described the sexual abuse perpetrated against her by her mother's violent partner.

"One night I woke up, and he was sitting on my bed... I was about 10. I'd just started to grow breasts... and he was going, 'Let me feel'.... I wouldn't let him. I was trying to turn over and go to sleep." (child)

It may be that significantly more than a quarter of the women in the survey had children who were also being abused by their violent partner. The declared figure of 27% may be depressed because of the mothers' reluctance to disclose the abuse or because of their ignorance of it. Or it may be because of the mothers' interpretation of the word 'abuse'. Certainly, in answer to another question, only 44% of mothers said that their violent partners 'didn't touch the children'.

Children witnessing their mothers being sexually abused

In answer to the question about the nature of the violence they experienced, 1 in 10 of the mothers (10%) reported that they had been sexually abused or assaulted by their violent partner in front of their children.

"I was raped once, in front of the children, with a knife at my throat. The children tried to pull him off, and it was just awful."

Children witnessing or overhearing violence

As Table 4 shows, almost three quarters (73%) of the children witnessed violent assaults on their mothers; and almost two thirds of them (62%) overheard violent incidents.

"He would come in and rip my mother's clothes off. He tried to strangle her, just beat her up like.... We were always watching it... he used to tell us to get back to bed... He would stamp on the phone so we couldn't phone the police." (child)

"It was worse seeing my mother hit than being hit myself." (child)

"He used to hit her in the street.... I'd be with her and he'd clobber her.... I'd just stick by her and cry.... that was when I was little." (child)

"Once, when I was about six, I saw my Dad throw my Mum across the room... my Mum shouted to my sister to take me upstairs.... I didn't want to leave her. I cried." (child)

"A lot of times I just heard it from my bedroom, and once (my sister)

and I heard it, and we were just crying our eyes out for my Mum, you know, she just sounded so desperate downstairs.... crying and screaming." (child)

"I know a couple of times my son must have witnessed it...a couple of times he's come up to me and said, 'Are you okay Mum'.... he was around when it happened."

"He smashed my head against the wall because (the baby) was making a mess. He picked up the dish and threw it at me and I was covered in baby food. I just collapsed on the floor. (The baby) was trying to pull me across the floor crying... saying, 'Mummy get up'."

Children witnessing the resulting injuries or seeing their mothers upset

More than half (52%) of respondents said that their children had witnessed the aftermath of violence or seen the resulting injuries. Almost all the mothers (99%) said that their children had seen them crying and upset after violent incidents.

"Another time he was beating my Mum up badly. I ran to get help, like, and the police came.... the next day... her face was just distorted you know, all black and blue, and she had stitches in her lip, and I think she had a fractured jaw... her neck was covered in love bites where he'd been strangling her." (child)

"My earliest memory was about the age of six.... I'd walk in, and she'd have a bloody nose or whatever, and she'd be crying all the time.... she told me it was an accident." (child)

"I think that he (my son) was aware of it because, you know, he would get up in the morning, and I would have a big black eye... They more or less accepted it... 'the usual thing', it didn't surprise them.... I don't think they liked it.... the fact that he was hurting me. But they never said anything."

Children aware of the atmosphere at home

As Table 4 shows, more than two thirds (69%) of women who said that they thought their children were aware of the violence at home said that this was because they believed that their children were aware of the atmosphere of fear and intimidation which was generated by their partner's violence. This can have as great an impact on children as on their mothers in terms of the inability to relax and enjoy life at home and the constant anxiety about what is going to happen next.

"We'd sit on hot bricks and wait for something to erupt."

"It was depressing. My mother was always on edge, scurrying around... And I was frightened as well, every time he was there, thinking, 'Oh, what's he going to do today? Is he going to knife her or what?'" (child)

"He just had like an aura around him, like it made you frightened all the time." (child)

"We would just sit there watching telly, and my Mum would be sitting there, and nobody would talk." (child)

In some cases, the violent partner's abuse of power and controlling behaviour extended to the children:

"It would be 11 o'clock at night... he wouldn't let my daughter go to bed. He made her just sit there all evening, and I kept saying to her to go to bed, and he'd say, 'She's not f...ing well going anywhere.... she will go when I tell her'. She got very upset and very tired, and he just got the lighter and lit the newspaper and was just putting the flames against me.... I had to keep pushing it away."

Children hurt 'by accident' during the course of attacks

More than a tenth (13%) of respondents said that their children had been hurt by accident during a domestic violence incident, having been "caught in the crossfire."

"He lobbed it (wooden block with knives) at the pantry door. It just missed the baby's head because he was standing over the cot."

"Me and my sister would jump on his back (to try to stop him hurting Mum), but he would just hit you off... and then you would go flying because he was so big."

Discussion: growing up in a violent situation – what it means to children

Given the nature, prevalence and severity of the violence experienced by many of the mothers in the survey, and the fact that in some cases men's violence was quite systematic and was sometimes either directed towards children or occurred in their presence, it is scarcely surprising that very few children of sufficient age were totally unaware of what was happening at home.

It is notable that all the children who were interviewed spoke with great feeling about their distress at witnessing their mothers' physical and emotional suffering. It is important not to underestimate the adverse effect of this on children who were, in many cases, quite young. Certainly, most of the children (and mothers) who were interviewed made it clear that their childhood experiences of violence, whether direct or otherwise, were very clearly etched on their memories and were indeed some of their clearest and earliest recollections. They often seemed to remember not only what they had seen (or experienced), but also how this had made them feel.

"I can remember what happened, and how it happened and stuff like that. You don't really lose it." (child)

"People think children are stupid, you know, like dumb animals, like the way they say, 'They're only young, it doesn't matter', but I'd say, kids, they know exactly what's going on." (child)

"They certainly remember my second husband, their step father. They have very, very vivid memories and pictures in their minds about what went on."

"My son will say, 'Remember that horrible man that used to live with us, and that day that he hit me with the belt, and you told him to leave me alone, and he beat you up?'... And I will say, 'How did you feel about it?' and he will say, 'Frightened'."

The vividness of these childhood memories helps to explain some of the findings reported in the following sections about the impact of domestic violence on the children.

4. The short term effects of domestic violence on children

Table 5 (below) illustrates the answers given by the mothers to the question about the nature of the short term effects of domestic violence on their children.

It is notable that more than 9 in 10 (91%) of the mothers believed that the violence had had some impact on their children in the short term. The remaining 9% was mainly comprised of those women whose children were babies at the time the violence had occurred.

Table 5: Short term effects of the violence on children

children's responses	%
children showed no reaction	9
frightened	72
very quiet	48
bed wetting problems	34
clung on to mother	63
tried to hide from violence	22
ran away	13
tried to protect their mother	31
tried to protect brothers and sisters	27
aggressive towards the violent partner	22
disobedient	36
aggressive towards their mother	25
aggressive to other children	30
difficulties with friends	21
problems at school	31

(96 respondents)

Children's fear and anxiety

'Being frightened' was the short term reaction to domestic violence most commonly reported of children by their mothers; almost three quarters (72%) of mothers said their children had reacted in this way.

Similarly, almost two thirds (63%) said that their children had become 'clingy'; almost half (48%) reported that their children were unnaturally quiet or withdrawn; and more than a third (34%) said that their children had developed bed wetting problems, they believed in response to the violence at home.

"During this period the children were absolutely terrified...you could see the terror in their faces. And they would say, 'Mummy, if he throws you out again tonight, please, please bring the police. Please don't leave us here alone with him."

"She would be very clingy, and even followed me to the toilet."

"They would wake up screaming and crying."

"(My daughter) was a bundle of nerves. She'd only have to see the car, and she'd be screaming in the street, 'Let's hide in here, Mum'... she was glued to me, and still is today."

"I don't sleep. I just mainly go to bed to be on my own and listen for when he comes in, and the only time I do eventually go to sleep is when

he's come in and I know he's alright with my Mum." (child)

Some of those who were interviewed made clear that children are sometimes scared that they will be the next target.

"(My daughter) would just sit there frozen. I mean, she didn't know what to do because if she got up to move... he would maybe have gone for her. So she was just, like, sitting there, trembling and crying and stuff."

"I just feel insecure myself, really, because I don't know whether one day my Mum's not going to be there, and he's going to turn round and have a go at me." (child)

Apart from bed-wetting problems, some of the children who were interviewed described other physical reactions to the violence at home.

"I wouldn't eat for weeks on end. And then he would make me eat, and I would go to the toilet and make myself sick. I lost a lot of weight, but I wasn't anorexic really because I would eat in school. I just wouldn't eat at home." (child)

"I kept on going to the toilet and everything like that." (child)

Withdrawing and running away

More than a fifth (22%) of mothers said they thought that their children had reacted to the violence by hiding; and more than a tenth (13%) said that their children had responded by running away.

"He (my son) used to run off and shut the door and cry."

"It was like my little safe house, that's where I felt safe – in my bedroom... no-one was allowed to come in my room." (child)

"We just try to keep out of his way, that's the best thing really." (child)

"I just put a barrier up against everyone around me... I'd just be in my bedroom all the time, playing with my toys or whatever. I just wouldn't want to see anyone." (child)

"(My sister) didn't know how to cope with it... she didn't know what to do with herself... she just locked herself away, like, in herself." (child)

Being protective of mothers, brothers and sisters, and aggressive towards violent partners

Almost a third (31%) of mothers said that their children had become protective towards them in the short term; and more than a quarter (27%) said that they had become protective of their brothers and sisters. More than a fifth (22%) of mothers said that their children had become aggressive towards their violent partner.

"I remember one occasion my brother was about two years old, and I came in from playing, and my mother was blue in the face, and my step-father had her by the throat, and I just - I don't know how I did it - I just remember running in the kitchen and grabbing a knife and going for him, but he moved, unfortunately." (child)

".... My mother sounded so desperate downstairs... crying and screaming.... he was a right pig, so we went downstairs with our tennis racquets and started hitting him." (child)

"If they'd start arguing and fighting, I just used to have my brother in my bedroom. I'd be like cuddling him and he'd be all upset." (child)

"I would take my little sister and brother upstairs... and I could hear everything he was saying, and I could hear my Mum crying and... I feel terrible because my sister and brother have to see it, knowing I've been through it, and I don't want them to be brought up like it.... if I take (my brother) up in my bedroom... and they're arguing, he'll sit there, and he'll cry his eyes out until my mother comes up." (child)

Some children fantasised about attacking their mother's violent partner.

"I remember doing little drawings, making little plans about how to kill my step-father and stupid things like that, pictures of knives and things." (child)

"My youngest will tell just anybody straight out what's been done to him and what his stepfather was like and fantastic fantasies about how he will do damage to him and how he wants other people to do damage to him."

Some children decided that their interventions during violent incidents could be counterproductive.

"I tried to stop him, but sometimes I used to think why stop him? Because he would only hit her once... but if we tried to stop him he'd go back for more and more, so sometimes I used to think, just leave him." (child)

Confronting the violence

Some of the mothers and children who were interviewed gave examples of the way in which the children had, very bravely, confronted their partner's violence, even though they were sometimes only young at the time. On occasions, they were able to protect their mothers simply through their refusal to leave them.

"One particularly violent incident, my son came in and intervened.... he just stood right beside me, and my husband had his hand up to hit me again, and (my son) just looked at him, and whatever it was, he stopped... I swear he would have killed me that day if it hadn't been for (my son)."

"I wanted to hear it, I wanted to hear what he was doing. I didn't want to be blind to what he was doing." (child)

"I remember (my daughter) saying to him once, 'This is my mother's house, and I don't want you in here, and you should get out'."

"He had his hands round my throat, and he was dragging me round the front room.... (my son) was screaming, trying to pull him off, so I sat down and then (the baby) woke up.... I sat on the settee with one either side, and I sort of cuddled them, trying to calm them down because they were both crying. And he came up and punched me really hard on the leg. He tried to pull the eldest away, but he wouldn't go, so I held on as tight as I could."

Children's aggression towards their mother and others

A quarter (25%) of mothers said that their children had responded to the violence in the short term by becoming aggressive towards them. In some cases it seems that this was because the children were generally angry and directed this towards everyone with whom they came into contact. Almost a third (31%) of mothers said that their children had also developed problems at school, and a similar proportion (30%) said that they had become aggressive towards other children. More than a third (36%) said that their children had become disobedient, and more than a fifth (21%) reported that the children had had difficulties with friends.

"I was angry with my father... And I took it out on my mother as well because she was still with him. I'd take it out on my brother as well.... there was no loving any more." (child)

"... the next thing (my son) would just run and attack (his sister) for no reason whatsoever."

In some cases, children said that they felt particularly frustrated with their mothers because of their apparent weakness and/or failure to protect themselves.

"I didn't want anything to do with my father, and I didn't want anything to do with my mother then, really, because she was leaving us to go through this, and watching her being beaten up every other day made me feel resentful.... I couldn't believe how stupid she was being." (child)

"I was very aggressive. I remember lashing out a few times at my mother...I used to swing for her all the time... I remember punching her in the face... I'd throw things at her... whatever was in my hand." (child)

"I rebelled against her because I didn't understand why she put us through it for so many years like.... I know she was going through the worst of it, but so were we. So I didn't understand why she did it to us... it would be on my mind at lot." (child)

Sometimes children believed that their mothers colluded with their violent partners in order to keep the peace.

"If I wanted to do something, she wouldn't let me do it because she knew that he'd disapprove, and she'd get it later from him... she just did it to sort of make the peace." (child)

"She wasn't able to do anything because she'd get hit herself." (child)

Children's embarrassment

Some children recalled events during which they had been embarrassed or ashamed of the violence at home.

"I used to think to myself, 'What's my friends at school going to say with my mother with all marks on her face.'" (child)

"I remember it was my tenth birthday party. I just remember being in the kitchen, crying my eyes out that he'd embarrassed me so much in front of my friends." (child)

"My friends have been there when he's hit my Mum... I mean, in front of me its not so bad, but he shouldn't do it in front of my friends." (child)

Children's confusion and emotional turmoil

Some of the children who were interviewed explained the confusion of emotions they felt because of the violence at home. Not least important was the feeling that they couldn't see an end to a horrible situation which they were powerless to change.

"I felt stunned basically – shocked, frightened, angry, everything. My head was just full of emotions. I just felt as though I was going to burst, you know, and it seemed like nothing could be done. It was there day in, day out. Nothing seemed to get better." (child)

Apart from feelings of fear and anger, some children said that they felt guilty, either because they believed that the violence was their fault, or because of how they had reacted to it.

"I would say to my mother, 'Can I stay up at my friend's house?' and my mother would say Yes. And then when I came home, I would have a row with my father because I hadn't asked him... that would cause an argument... if we caused an argument... you would go to bed and he would end up beating her about. You assumed it was your fault." (child)

"I was very aggressive....I used to swing for her all the time.... I remember punching her in the face.... sometimes I'd just head butt the walls. I thought I was going mad... and then I'd cry, just be really guilty for actually going for my own mother." (child)

The children who were interviewed had attempted to rationalise the violence. Different children came to different conclusions:

"I could never work out why my father would want to hit my mother about.... she would do nothing wrong. It was like she would come in and he would say she was a tart, and she would look really nice, and he would say to her, 'You're nothing but a tart, look at the way you dress', and he would rip her clothes off her... rip them to shreds." (child)

"There was one time, I thought it was all my Mum's fault he was hitting her all the time, but then to see it for myself and how he's treating me like, it's brought me and my Mum a lot closer." (child)

"I used to think that she hated me." (child)

"The violence made me hate him.... it upsets you doesn't it? You don't expect your father to hit your mother, do you? And I was always afraid of him." (child)

It is not surprising that some children simply become desperate.

"You come close to breaking point. I felt suicidal a lot of the time, but I never carried it through, thank God now, looking back." (child)

"I took an overdose when I was 16. That was when my mother really saw what was happening to me and what we were coming to.... it got to the stage when I just didn't want to live no more." (child)

"(My sister) does stupid stuff, like she lights a match, puts it out and burns her hand with it. And she's got scars on her arms." (child)

Comparing the short term effects of domestic violence on children who had also been abused by the violent partner, and those on 'child witnesses' of domestic violence

Cross-tabulations were computed to compare the short term effects of domestic violence on children according to whether or not the children themselves had also been hit or physically abused by their mother's violent partner. The base sample for this exercise comprised the children of 86 mothers, 23 of whose children had been abused by the violent partner and 63 of whose children had not.

The cross-tabulation showed that children who had also been abused were significantly more likely (ie. $p<.05$) to have reacted in the short term by being unnaturally quiet, by being aggressive to other children, by being disobedient and by having problems at school compared to children whose experience of violence was only indirect. (In the case of the latter two criteria, disobedience and problems at school, $p<.01$).

When considering these results it is important to remember that they are based on mother's perceptions of how their children had reacted in the short term, not on any scientific measures of children's emotional states or behaviour. Nonetheless, one might have expected to find that children who had been directly abused would have been much more badly affected compared to "child witnesses" of domestic violence than appears to be the case here. This in turn suggests that living in a home in which there is domestic violence may have a much more adverse impact on children in the short term than might otherwise have been supposed.

Discussion: the impact of domestic violence on children in the short term

The overwhelming majority of mothers who took part in the survey believed that the violence at home had made a serious impact on their children in the short term. This maternal perspective was reinforced by the views of the children (and mothers) who were interviewed.

Both the survey and the interview findings reported here suggest that domestic violence is a very profound experience for children who encounter it, whether directly or indirectly. It is important to stress that the great majority of children in this study did not seem able to "take the violence in their stride". They did not readily forget what they had seen, heard or felt.

In the short term, the violence at home appeared to have a serious impact on how the children perceived themselves, their mothers and the perpetrators of the violence, who were usually their fathers. The great majority of children were very frightened. Many children appeared to try to take some responsibility for what was happening and felt compelled to intervene in some way. Others were unable to do so and tended to 'shut themselves away', either physically, emotionally, or both. Some children became angry and more difficult to control, and problems quite often developed at school and with friends.

Most mothers said that they thought that their children had reacted to domestic violence in ways which appear at first to be conflicting - for example, by becoming aggressive both to them and to their violent partners. However, some of the comments from the children who were interviewed suggest why this may be. When trying to make sense of the violence, some children are filled with powerful and conflicting emotions which they find it almost impossible to reconcile.

"I love him in a way because he's my Dad.... he's what I've lived with all my life, but, I mean, I hate him for what he's done to my mother and put me through, and I just don't want him to put my brother and sister through it." (child)

The children who were interviewed all recalled having been shocked and confused at times by what was happening at home. These feelings may have been increased because most mothers in the survey tended not to discuss the violence with their children; fewer than a fifth (17%) of mothers said that they had done so. The lack of opportunity to talk about the violence sometimes added to children's feelings of resentment and isolation and meant that there was a "vacuum" which some children filled, as shown above, by believing that the violence was in some way their fault.

"I felt sort of pushed out, until she really sat down and told me, and then I sort of understood." (child)

"I think she thinks that I was too young to talk about it." (child)

Some of the mothers who were interviewed explained that they hadn't discussed the violence with their children, either because they were too busy trying to deal with their own problems to appreciate their children's emotional needs, or because they wanted to 'block it out'.

"Who is to say that at that time (my children) didn't feel that Mum's getting hit because of something I said or did, so they could have blamed themselves for what was happening to me, but I wouldn't have been aware of that, you see, because I was only too aware of what was going on with me and having to cope with what I was coping with."

"No, I never discussed it with (the children), and I think the reason was because of my own need to forget it and put it behind me. I didn't want it brought up.... I didn't want to talk to the children.... to anybody."

"My son was only very young.... I can't really remember. At the time I was under so much stress, I think I've pushed a lot of it out of my mind."

If mothers feel unable to discuss the violence with the children, it is unlikely that the children themselves will broach the issue. This may lead to a situation in which mothers feel - quite wrongly - that their children are silently siding with their violent partner against them.

"I didn't realise how good my son could be at covering things up. I didn't realise that he hated (my violent partner) as much as he did... I mean, he went along with everything."

However, the difficulties faced by mothers who do decide to discuss the violence with their children should not be underestimated.

"We could never talk because my mother and I used to just bawl out in tears." (child)

One of the reasons why domestic violence is confusing for children is because it is so complicated in terms of the effects that it has on all the relationships within a family. Experiencing violence often has a very significant impact on women's ability to perform the role of a mother, and this in turn impacts back on the children and on their feelings about their mother, her violent partner and themselves.

This is an important added dimension to understanding the nature and severity of the short term impact of domestic violence on children, and it is examined in the next section.

5. The short term effects of domestic violence on mothers

More than four fifths (84%) of mothers said that they felt that their children were harder to look after when the violence was happening. This was thought to be for the reasons set out below.

Table 6: Reasons why mothers believed their children were harder to look after when there was violence at home

Reasons	% answering yes
children more difficult	38
children aggressive	34
children refused to listen	34
children afraid	40
mother physically injured	28
mother afraid	61
mother depressed	76
mother exhausted	55

(105 respondents)

Note: percentages add to more than 100 because most respondents answered yes to several categories.

Clearly, in the view of most mothers, their children were more difficult to look after at this time in no small part because of the impact of the violence on the children's well being and behaviour, as described in some detail in the previous section and as reflected again in the first four categories in Table 6.

The other dimension which is important to take into account is the effect of the violence on the women as mothers. This factor is reflected in the last four categories of Table 6 and is the focus of this section.

More than three quarters (76%) of mothers said that they thought that the fact that they were depressed affected their parenting; approaching two thirds (61%) believed that their own fear was an important factor, and more than half (55%) identified being exhausted as an adverse influence. Rather fewer, just over a quarter (28%) thought that they had found it harder to look after their children because they had been physically injured.

It is notable that most mothers seemed to believe that the problems they experienced in caring for their children were due more to the impact of the violence on them, rather than on their children. It is also interesting that most mothers clearly felt that it was the emotional rather than the physical effects of domestic violence which most impaired their parenting at this time. Comments from the women who were interviewed suggest that this may often have been because of the way in which the violence had systematically disempowered them.

Depression and stress-related illnesses

On the whole, the mothers who were interviewed spoke very frankly about their concerns over the inadequate care they often felt they had given their children when they were coping with violence from their partner. Some of them spoke of depression and stress-related illnesses brought on by the violence absorbing almost all of their energies.

"I used to cry a lot. I was really depressed. I was in and out of hospital with stress related illnesses."

"I was in a hell of a state. I was in bandages for about eighteen months with my hands, with my nerves. I came out in a nervous rash."

"I was so wound up in this relationship, and I was depressed... there just wasn't any energy for my son, and I was so distracted."

"I made myself housebound. Eighteen months I was in my house, and I wouldn't go outside the gate."

Mothers' lack of self-confidence

Many of the mothers said that their experience of violence had eroded their self-esteem, not least their confidence in their parenting abilities. Sometimes their partners had made matters worse not only by their actions but also by deliberately undermining them in their role as parents.

"I was a nervous wreck. I was just like a gibbering idiot. I had no confidence, no self esteem. I thought I was the most useless thing... because when you are being told all the time that you are crap, you sort of eventually begin to believe it."

"I felt so useless, and if you're going through a situation like that you begin to believe that that's what you are, and that's all the good you are."

"You lose your self-esteem, you lose trust.... you're practically left with nothing."

"He (my partner) always used to say I was a bad mother... my way of

coping was to start drinking, not to the level of an alcoholic, but it wasn't very good... he used to tell everyone how awful I was."

"He had a probation officer.... they were trying to blame me all the time.... I don't know what he told them, but I was the one seen to be the bad one...I always had the children. He was never there. So how could I be an unfit mother... he was the one who was beating me up."

"I haven't been able to talk to my children either. I haven't been able to play games with them like normal parents do.... I can't do simple things like that."

Nothing left emotionally to give the children

Most of the mothers who were interviewed said that they had never compromised their children's physical welfare by neglecting them, at least not consciously. However, they often admitted that because they were shocked, depressed or exhausted by the violence, they had very little to give their children emotionally. The mothers frequently felt guilty, distressed or angry about this.

"I was crying... in the kitchen doing dinner.... crying all the time.... I was like a robot. It was like I got up in the morning, my switch was turned on, and it was turned off again at the end of the day, and those days and weeks and months that went past, I couldn't really tell you what happened from day to day."

"You just feel like a zombie and you just do it...you wake up in the morning... wishing that you never had to start the day...."

"You put a protective barrier around yourself that stops you from completely crumbling... there was no room for that extra cuddle.."

"I always tried to be a good Mum... regular school attendance... fed every day... clean clothes, baths... but that was it, that was as much as I could do. There was nothing left to talk about... emotionally, it was almost like I'd had enough."

"I wanted to look after my son properly... not that he was neglected in any way... but I was too distracted to look after him in the way that he deserved."

"I felt guilty about my son not having proper care."

"I'm very angry because the violence took away the first two years when I could have enjoyed my son."

Some of the children who were interviewed showed that they had been aware of their mothers' state of mind.

"The violence was draining her.... she had no personality...s he just wasn't happy." (child)

Mothers neglecting their own and their children's physical needs

Although most of the mothers who were interviewed said that they had been able to continue to care for their own and their children's physical needs despite the violence, several mothers admitted that there had been times when they became so depressed that they had become unable even to do this.

"I just didn't care. He was so cruel that I didn't take any pride in myself.... I lost the baby.... I was only seven stone."

"At one time I went through a depression that went on for about a year where I didn't bother do the housework, and I didn't bother to wash myself... I didn't give a shit about who said what about how the children looked... People must have known, people must have seen the way I was looking and the way the children were looking.... but it's almost like once you get yourself into that, it's like you just sit and watch it."

Some of the children who were interviewed gave examples of how there had been periods when they had been 'neglected', although these disclosures were usually followed by them pointing out the pressures their mothers were under at the time.

"We never had breakfast, ever, when we was little. Never had lunch. We just had dinner.... but the kids have breakfast now... they're alright now because my Mum's grown up a lot as well, and she's a good mother, she really is now.... I was supposed to have gone round to the shop on my way to school." (child)

"My mother went really bad... she was like seven stone, and she was really thin. She drank a lot.... every night she would... come home paralytic. It was her way of blocking it out... She tended to give us a lot of love, but it wasn't in the ways we needed it... She wasn't there for you all the time... because she would be out drinking. And it was all her problems... she never had a lot of time for you." (child)

One child who was interviewed, an adolescent girl whose mother was still living with her violent partner, seemed to have taken on many of the tasks of caring for her younger brother and sister.

"I'm worn out at the end of the day... I'm awful overworked really... On weekends I get up for the two little ones, and I'm constantly making tea from the time I get out of bed.... I've been through a lot for my age because I used to have them in my bedroom with me when they were little, while my mother would be sitting downstairs, so tired, not going to bed, not knowing what he was going to do to her... hit her or something." (child)

Mothers taking out their frustrations on the children

Some of the mothers who were interviewed explained that they had sometimes taken out the anger and frustration they felt towards their partners on their children. This was sometimes compounded by the behaviour of their children who they were finding more difficult to manage, or by the feeling that their violent partner had much more authority over the children than they did.

"I've also had difficulties with controlling my own temper... My mind just conks out and all I'm filled with is anger – anger and bitterness and frustration, especially when things are going wrong, and I'm worrying about something else, and I take it out on the kids.... I hit them.... but now I can feel it coming, and I'm able to ring someone now and speak to them about it."

"It gets harder – like the more hassle you have, you seem to divert it onto the kids. A lot of the time (my son) would be getting hit just because he was his father's son, and I used to think... I shouldn't take it out on him, because its not his fault... I think, 'Well, I've only done that because (my violent partner) is getting at me, and I'm taking it out on them because I can't take it out on him'."

"I haven't got a lot of patience at the moment. I tend to have a go at them for a lot of things which I don't really mean to do. I lose my temper quite quickly."

"I could tell them off ten times, till I get a sore throat in the end or something, but he's only got to say it once and they listen, and it gets me going."

One of the children who was interviewed explained that her mother managed to control her temper much better now that she was no longer living with her violent partner.

"I used to get belted, but... she doesn't hit the kids any more. She doesn't smack any more. She tries to deal with it in a calmer way." (child)

Discussion: domestic violence can divide mothers from their children in the short term

Some of the mothers and children who were interviewed helped to fill in the complex emotions lying behind the deceptively simple survey finding that, 'Four in five of the mothers found their children more difficult to look after when they were experiencing violence from their partner'.

The key factors which the women and children identified were the exhaustion and depression which mothers felt and their self-absorption. A comment from one mother suggested that she was so focussed on her own needs at this time that she was unable to safeguard her child from possible harm.

"He used to like to keep my son up late and liked to sleep with him. I used to pray that he would take him to bed because I hated the thought of him coming to bed with me.... Quite often he would force me to have sex with him." (She reported that on at least one occasion her violent partner had picked up her son in a fit of anger and thrown him across the room, but she gave no indication of concern that he might have sexually abused her son.)

All too often, mothers had no emotional space for their children, who consequently tended to feel 'shut out' and resentful, even if they could understand why their mothers were behaving as they did. These feelings could lead the children, in turn, to become more difficult to manage, which of course simply compounded the problems which mother and children were experiencing together.

"I feel pushed out in a way.... Many times I just go up in my bedroom, and I sit down and cry."(child)

"I just couldn't show her my feelings... I felt resentment towards her for putting him before me and my brother, which she did.... Don't tell her. It was only because she wanted to please my Dad all the time..... but he didn't do much for her.... He never complimented her or spoke to her in a nice way. It was always nastiness and putting her down so that she didn't feel good about herself, like taking away her confidence." (child)

The sadness is that it was at this time that mothers and children probably most needed each others' support and yet were often least able to provide it. In this sense, domestic violence sometimes seems to 'divide and rule' within a family, leaving all the victims - the mothers and their children - feeling isolated and unhappy.

6. The longer term effects of domestic violence on children

More than four fifths (86%) of mothers said that they thought that there had been long-lasting effects on their children as a result of them experiencing domestic violence.

One mother who was interviewed explained how she felt the violence had affected her children as they grew up.

"I don't think it comes out when they are children... it starts to show from adolescence... because they start becoming more confident themselves.... the anger starts to come out and they do start to question as well. I didn't sort of automatically think, 'Oh well, this is because they witnessed me getting a good kicking so many years previously.' I thought, "My God, is this what teenage years are going to be like – its going to be hell!"'

It is notable that some of the mothers who were interviewed said that the children had very clear memories of the violence they had experienced and how this had made them feel. All of the children interviewed confirmed this (see also section 3, discussion, above).

"They remember the black eyes, and they remember the beatings, fighting, the arguing – they remember it all."

"I still think about it a lot now." (child)

One child who was interviewed said that she had made a positive effort not to remember what had happened.

"I've blocked it out... that's the only way I deal with things really." (child)

Clearly, then, domestic violence 'matters' a great deal to most children who experience it, and this sets the context for the findings about mothers' views of the long term impact of domestic violence on children, set out below in Table 7.

Table 7: longer term effects of the violence on children

children's reactions	%
no long-lasting effects	14
violent or aggressive	33
harder to control	33
full of anger and bitterness	29
defensive and protective	28
lacks respect for mother	21
lacks self-confidence	31
sad and withdrawn	18
problems trusting people	24

(100 respondents)

Violence and aggression

A third of the mothers (33%) said that they believed that their children were violent or aggressive in the long term because of the violence. The same proportion (33%) said that they thought their children were harder to control. These were the two criteria by which most mothers chose to describe the long term impact of the violence on their children.

"Both my sons are very aggressive and very violent.... the youngest boy even more so than his older brother. His anger has come more towards me and towards anybody else who gets in his way, really. He just belts them really hard.... The youngest one's got a lot of hate in him, a great deal of hate....He's got this thing about being hard, and, you know, he's a man now... I think he needs a good kick up the backside."

"His temper just seems to have got worse... you'll say something and he'll just blow – have a full paddywhack, and then you just have to leave him to calm down."

"(My sister) went sort of haywire.... and (my brother) went very nasty.... if you were in a room with him, he would run up to you and punch you, and he would laugh because he thought it was right." (child)

Bitterness and blame

Nearly a third (29%) of mothers said they thought that their children were filled with anger and bitterness in the long term as a result of their experiences of domestic violence.

"They'll say to me now, 'Oh I hate you....I want to go and live with my Dad'. 'Go and live with your bloody father then.' I say. My son says to me, 'Anyway, its all your fault that I wasn't at school'..... Whether he

blames me for the trouble he's been in I don't know. But sometimes I get the feeling that he does, because I left his Dad, even though he knows what his Dad's like."

"My daughter gets moody... she's down your throat, she'll shout at you... she is impossible to get along with, she's just really, really awful."

"(My daughter) once said to me, 'My attitude to life is look after number one and to hell with everybody else'."

"It isn't getting much of a childhood. I went without a childhood." (child)

Being protective and feeling guilty

More than a quarter of the mothers (28%) said that they thought that in the longer term the violence had made their children defensive and protective. Some of the women and children who were interviewed gave examples of this from their own lives, particularly so far as the desire of children to protect their mothers from possible harm was concerned.

"I don't know if he understood at the time. He comes out with things now like, 'Oh, when I get bigger my daddy's never going to hit you again, because.... I can look after you.'"

"My daughter she says, 'Oh, I'll never leave you Mum.' I says 'Why?' She says, 'Well, what are you going to do, just you and him then?', because she goes mad, like, if he starts.... she's awful protective, she's like glue to me."

"If me and (my new boyfriend) have a row, she'll usually go up and punch him and swear at him... she doesn't swear normally... If there is an argument, she'll punch hell out of him... she's run out of the house crying.... she rung the police once... I think she told them that he was going to kill me."

"I go to bingo twice a week, and she'll come up and meet me. She'll be outside.... she's very clingy."

Comments from the mothers, and especially from the children who were interviewed, suggest that when children reflected back on the violence they often felt guilty because of their actions, or because they felt they should have done more to protect their mothers at the time. These feelings may have contributed to their desire to protect their mothers now.

"I didn't show my mother much affection as a child." (child)

"My son feels that a lot of it was his fault."

"I should have been more protective to my mother I think.... well, I just should have been there more for her when she was going through it. I know I was younger, but I don't know, I think I should have helped my brother a bit more." (child)

Lacking respect for their mothers

More than a fifth of the mothers (21%) said that they thought that in the longer term their children lacked respect for them as a result of the violence.

"My daughter treats me with total disrespect.... maybe its because I warranted it and I used to think, 'Well, maybe its the backlash of what happened, and maybe I've just got to bite my tongue and take it'."

"My daughter once said to me, 'When I'm an adult.... I don't want to be you..... because when I've seen everything that you've gone through, believe me, that's not going to happen to me'."

For two of the mothers who were interviewed, their sons' disrespect seemed to be in danger of escalating into violence.

"My eldest son is getting to look like his father.... he's gobby like their side of the family.... they treat their women as if they're just there to keep the house tidy and look after the kids.... he's got the same kind of attitude.... we have a lot of conflict with him now.... he'll threaten me, but I mean he's littler than me.... You can see it, though, sometimes in him that he wants to hit me...whether its just that I'm his mother, or that he's frightened of me that explains why he doesn't, but there'll be a time when he gets past that and thinks, 'Well I'm just going to sock her one.'.... I am frightened of him when he threatens me, but I think, 'No, I'm not going to let you know I'm frightened'."

"My oldest son's smashed my house up... personal things that he knows mean something to me, and he does it to his brother's things and to his sister's things. Both boys are filled with anger, and its hard for me because I think, 'Why the hell should I put up with the damage that someone else has done to my kids?'"

Feeling sad and lacking self-esteem

Almost a fifth of the mothers (18%) said that they thought that their children were sad and withdrawn, and almost a third (31%) said that they thought their children lacked self-confidence as long term results of the violence at home.

"The kids have been affected by him hitting me all the time... now, if there is a raised voice in the family, my younger daughter shakes, she cries, she runs out of the house.... I think she's mentally scarred by it."

"My son seems to keep things to himself. He's a sensitive child anyway, but he seems to cry at the slightest little thing."

"My daughter has no confidence whatsoever.... she struggles all the way down the line."

"When all the kids are playing, I watch my son.... he's not as outgoing, he's getting better all the time, but if anybody talks to him in the street he'll not answer them.... it was very bad when we first left."

"I don't know whether (my younger brother) remembers it, but he's a nervous child.... if you (go near him), he thinks you're going to hit him.... he must remember it.... he has nightmares a lot and everything." (child)

"My confidence at the moment is really bad... I don't show it... I just have this really low opinion of myself where he made me feel shit... so I believed it in the end." (child)

"I think, 'Well, why should I tidy myself up, I'm not going nowhere?'." (child)

"I went to secondary school... going in dressed like a tramp and just not having much respect for myself, no one else respected me you know... " (child)

Relationships with other people

Almost a quarter of mothers in the survey (24%) said that they thought that their children had problems in trusting other people as a longer term effect of the violence they had experienced at home. Some of the mothers, and almost all of the children, who were interviewed gave examples of this from their own lives.

"There was no conversation from (my daughter) at all. She seemed to back away from people."

"I mean people have asked me out and I think, 'Well no, is he going to be like what my Dad's like to my Mum?', and in the end it stops me from seeing my friends because they all go out with boys." (child)

"I always used to say that I would never stick for it being done to me.... I wouldn't trust anybody, like. My mother, she is just married to another man. I wouldn't trust him.... We hate each other to this day. because I

have never trusted him.... It just makes you wary of people.... because you think to yourself, 'He could turn out like him'." (child)

".... I think I'm afraid of being hurt, and I've always got that picture of my mother in the back of my mind being beaten up, and I think, 'Oh, all men are like that, that's gonna happen to me'." (child)

"I thought to myself, 'I'm never going to get married.'... I always thought..... 'Start seeing a boy and all that, they do the same as your father did'." (child)

Some of the children and mothers who were interviewed spoke of how 'hard' and self-contained the children had been forced to become to cope with their childhood experiences. As they grew older, this was having an impact on their capacity to be close to other people.

"I think it made (my daughter) so independent because she had to be strong as a child, because with everything going on with me, I really didn't have time... to worry.... it was enough to get them clean, washed, fed and do all the stuff you have to do as a Mum, but when you've got children that are watching as well..... she became very hard and strong in herself to survive."

"What (the violence) did take away from me is my femininity... I was always a dainty little girl until I was about six... but then I just started having to be hard all the time.... If I was this dainty little girl, I'd have no chance, really, would I?.... I'd be vulnerable." (child)

"I still now find it hard to leave myself go completely, because of thinking, you know, of all the things that have happened." (child)

"I can't stand people around me all the time. I like my own space." (child)

"I just got really hard and now I can't show my feelings to anyone.... I always have to have this front for people.... I can't put it down.... I won't get myself in a situation where I can be hurt, really." (child)

"There is a barrier around me and I won't let anybody in." (child)

Comparing the longer term effects of domestic violence on children who had also been abused by the violent partner, and those on 'child witnesses' of domestic violence

Cross-tabulations were carried out to compare the longer term effects of domestic violence on children, depending on whether or not the children themselves had also been hit or abused by the mother's violent partner. The base sample for this exercise comprised the children of 86 mothers, 23 of whose children had been abused by their violent partner and 63 of whose children had not.

The cross-tabulation showed that children who had themselves been abused by their mother's violent partner were significantly more likely (ie. $p<.05$) to have reacted in the longer term by being violent and aggressive, by lacking self-confidence, by having problems in trusting other people and by being angry and bitter compared with children who had experienced domestic violence less directly. (In the case of the latter two criteria, having problems in trusting other people and being angry and bitter, $p<.01$).

As when considering the results of the cross-tabulation carried out concerning the short-term impact of violence on children, it is important to note that these findings are based on the mothers' perceptions of how their children had reacted in the short-term, not on objective measures of the young people's behaviour and well being. Nonetheless, despite this caveat, again it is perhaps surprising that greater differences did not emerge between the responses of children who had themselves been abused compared with those who had not. Again, this tends to suggest that the longer term effects of domestic violence on children who are not themselves abused are greater than might otherwise be supposed.

Growing up away from their mothers

More than one in eight (13%) of the mothers who took part in the survey said that they had other children who were not living with them as a direct result of the domestic violence they had experienced. (Note: these children were therefore in addition to the 246 who formed the sample for the survey).

Six of these mothers had children accommodated by the local authority (one in residential care and five fostered); three women had children who were living with other relatives; and five had children who were living with their ex-partner, all as a direct result of the violence.

Growing up away from their mothers clearly constituted a profound impact of domestic violence for the children concerned.

Disrupted education

The survey did not include a question about the impact of domestic violence on children's education, but comments from some of the mothers and children who were interviewed show that violence at home can seriously damage the quality of children's educational experiences and outcomes.

Children's education can be disturbed by domestic violence in a number of different ways. Firstly, and most obviously, children who are living in a violent situation may be so distracted and distressed that they are unable to concentrate on studying at school.

"His work is suffering at school... his reading is suffering... he can't concentrate."

"From the age of eleven, I truanted sometimes. I couldn't concentrate on my studies. I just couldn't do a lot of things... I couldn't focus." (child)

"It got so bad I had to go to special classes... I found it so hard to concentrate.... they always thought I was slow." (child)

"You don't concentrate a lot, like, if it happened in the night and I was in school. You would be upset in the day. And somebody would say something to me, and I would just cry and stuff like that." (child)

A second way in which long term damage may be done to children's education, even if their experience of domestic violence is relatively short-lived, is if children get out of the habit of being in school, or feel that, having missed some time, they cannot catch up, or that school no longer has anything to offer them. Clearly, if children do not attend school, they are unlikely to obtain any educational qualifications, and their job prospects will suffer accordingly.

"She lost a lot of schooling. Still today she don't go to school.... she says, 'What else can they learn me?'.... From the age of four and a half when she started school, she was very rarely there because I used to be frightened to go and get her from school (because of my violent partner)."

"For the last two years (my son) ain't been to school... he got out of the habit when he went to live with his Dad, because like he weren't bothered what he did.... he more or less looked after himself."

One child, still living in a violent situation, who was interviewed gave a further example of how children's education can be disrupted by domestic violence.

"I pick up all the work and do it at home. I'd rather do it at home than at school because then I know that if anything happened to my Mum I'd be there with her.... I think well, 'If I'm there I can pick up my brother and sister if she's too upset to go to the school'." (child)

Leaving home

The survey did not include a question about whether mothers thought that domestic violence had affected, or would affect, their children's decisions about leaving home as young adults. However, some of the mothers and children who were interviewed made clear that the violence at home had influenced children's decisions about when to leave home.

It is entirely natural for young people to leave their parental home and to establish an independent lifestyle, and the average age for leaving home in Britain is twenty three. However, it is also important that young people are able to plan when they strike out on their own so that they have somewhere to go and enough money to support themselves. There is a danger that children living in violent situations may leave home prematurely, with insufficient resources, or be thrown out by one or other parent. In these circumstances, homelessness may be the result.

If children leave home and things do not work out, they may need to return home to regather their material and emotional resources before setting out again on their own. However, young people who leave home prematurely in response to violence may be unable to return to their parents.

Certainly, two of the children who were interviewed, who were now being helped by NCH Action For Children projects for young people who were homeless or in housing need, had left home in direct response to family violence.

"I left home at 16. I just put my trainers on, went down to my sister's.... the police came and they...made sure that my father didn't come near me.... I said to my mother that I was going. She said, 'You go and you won't come back.' I said I didn't care." (child)

The decision of one of these children to leave home was more a response to her mother's behaviour rather than to the violent relationship itself which by now was over.

"I rebelled against my mother... at the age of 15 or 16... she threw me out in the end.... Well, she got into a relationship with my step father, who beat her up, and then, a couple of months later she got into a relationship with (a new boyfriend)... I just didn't like the way she was.... I have to be honest.... my mother has always thought about her men... her men come first.... I just blamed her for getting another man. I don't see how she could have done it." (child)

Another child who was interviewed explained that as a teenager she had gradually drifted away from her home and her parents.

"I went out a lot with friends, stayed overnight... that caused a lot of friction... (my mother) really held that against me... but it was because my friends always showed me more than what my family ever did." (child)

Children who are very protective may feel that they are unable to leave home unless, or until, they are sure that their mothers or other members of the family are safe.

"I'd have to make sure my Mum was alright before I left home.... I wouldn't leave home if he was still doing it to my Mum because it is my sister and brother that wouldn't benefit from it." (child)

Similarly, some mothers may be so reliant on their children for support that they find it impossible to 'let their children go.'

"I said to my mother, I wanted to leave home.... she said, 'Well, I don't want you to leave home.... because you're all I've got... you're my peace to fall back on. I can always turn around and take you upstairs and talk to you'. I mean, my Mum has always been able to talk to me... whatever she says to me won't go no further." (child)

Discussion: the longer term impact of domestic violence on children's lives

The great majority of mothers in the survey believed that their children's experiences of violence at home had seriously affected their children in the long term, and all the mothers and children who were interviewed tended to support this view. Certainly, this study contains abundant evidence in support of the notion that domestic violence is often a very significant experience for children, and one which produces long term as well as short term effects.

Very similar proportions of mothers thought that their children had become violent or aggressive, harder to control, bitter, defensive, and lacking in self-confidence as a result of their experience of domestic violence. The comments of mothers and children who were interviewed suggest that domestic violence may in some cases cast a long shadow over children's ability to form appropriate personal relationships as young adults.

There was also some compelling qualitative research evidence in the study to support the view that domestic violence may also have a significant impact on children's longer term life chances, in terms of their educational attainments and their ability to leave home in a planned, supported way. The immediate impact of domestic violence may be to make children more aggressive or more withdrawn, but the later, disastrous outcome for these children as young adults may be that at sixteen or seventeen they have no qualifications and poor employment prospects and have become homeless and estranged from their families.

However, it is clear that not all children are affected equally in the long term with respect either to the severity of the impact or its nature, and anecdotal evidence suggests that some children may be scarcely affected at all. As is invariably the case in the social sciences, it is almost impossible to say why some children are affected more profoundly than others, and since this study did not seek to control all the possible variables, there is no definitive 'answer' to this question contained within the research.

However, as one of the most reflective mothers who was interviewed observed from her own personal experience, key factors may include children's personalities and their innate capacity for resilience.

"(My oldest daughter) had something there and she was a real extrovert.... she had this sort of stable network... that helped her through them years... but (the violence) had an opposite effect on (her younger sister)... she didn't have a lot of friends... she has difficulty making friends, and when she does have friends they don't last long.... (my oldest daughter) was always a confident child anyway, you know, she was just a very confident young girl, and she was always able to talk to anybody."

It seems highly likely that another key variable in determining the longer term outcomes for children who experience domestic violence is the quality of the relationship which children are able to maintain with their mothers. Findings reported in previous sections have already suggested that domestic violence may have a serious impact on this relationship in the short term.

Moreover, a third (33.1%) of the mothers who took part in the survey said that they believed that their children were harder (for them) to control in the longer term; more than a fifth (21%) of mothers said that they felt that their children lacked respect for them in the longer term; and one in eight !3%) of the mothers had other children living completely apart from them – all as direct results of the violence.

The issue of the impact of domestic violence on women as mothers is the focus of the next section.

7. The longer term effects of domestic violence on mothers

The survey did not include a question asking women to comment on how, if at all, domestic violence had impacted on their role as mothers in the longer term. However, the mothers and children who were interviewed suggested that domestic violence may affect the longer term relationships between mothers and children in various ways. This short section examines ways in which the relationship between mothers and children may be affected by the impact of the violence on the mothers themselves.

Lack of self-confidence as women and mothers

Some women who experience domestic violence are left in the longer term feeling generally demoralised and depressed. One mother who was interviewed, who was still living with a violent partner, described her feelings of hopelessness and of having lost her opportunity of having a happy and fulfilling life.

"My daughter very often says to me, 'Wouldn't it be nice Mum, if we were on our own?', and I say, 'Don't keep on about it, because it could never be.'.... When I look back now I could kick myself, I think he ruined me, ruined my life.... he was my first man and my last.... He's just been pestering me ever since. I don't seem to go up the ladder, I never will, but then I think, 'Well, I've got nobody, no family'...."

As has been discussed in a previous section, more than a fifth (21%) of mothers who took part in the survey thought that in the longer term their children had less respect for them as a result of the domestic violence.

"My daughter treats me with total disrespect.... maybe its because I warranted it and I did used to think, 'Well, maybe its the backlash of what happened, and maybe I've just got to bite my tongue and take it'."

In some cases, their children's actions or words served simply to reinforce the poor opinion the women had already formed of themselves as both people and mothers.

"Sometimes you feel like maybe I'm not being a good mum."

"I actually started to think there was something wrong with me... it must be me. How can this happen to me twice... are there certain women that attract abusers?"

Feeling that they had let their children down may have contributed to mothers' low self-esteem, especially if in retrospect they had come to appreciate that their attention had been very much on themselves when they had been in the violent relationship rather than on their children.

"I didn't even take into consideration, not once, how it was affecting the girls.... I was too busy... they had a lot materially.... my father lavished everything on the girls, so they got the latest bikes and they got lots of toys.... maybe in thinking that they had that, that they were fine, (I didn't) deal with the emotional side of what they could be going through."

Emotional distance between mothers and children

Several of the mothers who were interviewed indicated that they thought that the domestic violence had permanently damaged their ability to form and sustain loving relationships with other people, including, in some cases, their children.

"I don't know how its going to affect any of us, but I think it has left me less loving, definitely, as a person, even towards my own children.... a harder person.... I'm not a person now for cuddles because it has destroyed the best side of me, I think, that I can never find again."

Since some of the children who were interviewed explained that they too felt they had become 'harder', and as comparatively few mothers and children seem to feel able to discuss the violence, it is not surprising that some of the mothers who were interviewed described their relationships with their children as being characterised by emotional distance.

"(There's a distance between us now) because I can remember being more close to them as babies, definitely."

"My son and I drew apart. We ended up seeing a family counsellor... he had a social worker because we'd drawn so far apart... he was going into his world, I was going into my world, and it was terrible, it was as if I had a complete stranger with me... I was frightened to say anything to him, and he was frightened to say anything to me... in the end we weren't saying anything."

"After the break up (my children and I) weren't connecting very well, and there were lots of ups and downs."

"Because there was so much going on with my own personal life... I've tended to push my oldest son away, and it's been very difficult to build the bonds between us."

Mothers' fears for their children's futures

Several of the mothers interviewed expressed anxiety about what would happen to their children in the future because of their childhood experiences of domestic violence. Their concerns tended to focus on worries about their children copying the behaviour they had seen – with girls becoming frightened of men or overcompliant, and boys violent and aggressive towards women.

"I'm very afraid for (my daughter). I mean, I know, or at least I hope, that she'll never suffer the abuse I have, and that she doesn't get sexually abused or anything like that, and that she'll be aware of men like that and the way that men are..."

"I do worry about their adult relationships because I do wonder what they will tolerate...I have actually said to them, 'No man has any right to lay his hand on any woman!'"

"I don't want (my sons) to grow into men like their fathers were."

"I didn't want my daughter growing up terrified that all men were like that, and (my son) thinking that that is the way you treat women...."

Several of the mothers who were interviewed certainly seemed to subscribe to the gender stereotypes of how children respond to stress at home, with boys externalising and girls internalising their problems.

"I often wonder if it's because they're a different sex, because if they were boys I think it would be a completely different story... with boys they would be violent, definitely, and they would have behavioural problems and they would be stealing and doing things."

One mother who was interviewed believed that her young son was growing up to be like the other men in her family – dominant and aggressive, and she was quite sure that he would eventually become violent towards her like his father had.

"He's getting to look like him... he's gobby like their side of the family... they treat their women as if they're just there to keep the house tidy and to look after the kids... he's got the same kind of attitude... there'll come a time when he thinks, 'Well, I'm just going to sock her one'..."

It is possible that some mothers who have suffered domestic violence may come almost to 'expect' their sons to behave in an aggressive way like their fathers. This may have an impact on how they treat their sons, and on how their sons learn to behave.

".... A lot of the time (my son) would be getting hit just because like he were his father's son, kind of thing, and I used to think, 'I shouldn't take it out on him, its not his fault'."

Similarly, some mothers may become so anxious about their daughters that they become over-protective of them.

Discussion: mothers as well as their children may need help to overcome the longer term effects of domestic violence

There was a prevailing sense of regret and of something good having been lost forever when some of the mothers who were interviewed spoke about the longer term effects of domestic violence on themselves and their children. Several mothers seemed to believe that they had completely failed their children, that the domestic violence was 'their fault' and that they were not very successful in any aspect of their lives, thereby completely underestimating their own resilience and strength in 'surviving' some very difficult and damaging experiences.

Findings reported in previous sections have shown how children may be left feeling angry, bitter and confused by the violence they have experienced. Some of the children who were interviewed commented on how they felt deprived of a childhood by the violence they had experienced at home, not least because they had been forced to confront at a very young age some very painful realities in terms of how the adults who mattered to them most felt and behaved. It is, therefore, probably not surprising that emotional distance characterised the relationships between some mothers and children in the longer term.

Overall, then, a picture emerges of some mothers and children being left feeling uneasy and unhappy together as a result of the domestic violence; and of some mothers in particular being very worried and anxious about their children's prospects and abilities to form appropriate relationships with other people.

It would, therefore, seem that many mothers and their children would benefit from professional help in overcoming together the effects of the domestic violence they have experienced. In fact, many of the mothers who expressed such concerns and unhappiness were being helped to recover from the effects of domestic violence by the NCH Action For Children family centre with which they were in contact (as is explained in a later section).

8. Leaving a violent partner

The question 'why don't they leave?' is often asked about women living with violent partners. This section aims to answer this question, drawing on both quantitative and qualitative data from the study.

Leaving and going back

More than four fifths (84% – 90 out of 107) of mothers in the survey had left home because of the violence, many on numerous occasions. Of those who gave a numerical answer to the number of times they had left, on average they had left 4.3 times, but the range was from 1 to 20 times.

Many of the women who took part in the survey had, therefore, left temporarily, but had then resumed their lives with the violent partner. Often this was because their violent partners had forced their way back, regardless of whether or not the woman had obtained injunctions designed to keep them away.

"He was given a week to get out of here. I rang the police to come here with me to check whether he had gone or not.... When I came down, there was no police... there was no sign of him....I moved myself and the children back in. I went down to the shop to get a pint of milk, and when I came back up the road he was inside the house... I was too afraid to go to the phone.... I took him back through fear."

"I used to take him back.... he used to kick the door in... at two or three in the morning."

"Another time I tried to leave, I went to a friend's house with everything piled up in the buggy... he caught me and took the eldest child back.... Everything happened so fast you know... (my son) was being dragged this way and that."

"My Mum had loads of injunctions against himl, and he broke in a few times and smashed the place up." (child)

Other women admitted that they lacked the resolve to go through with leaving their partner and their home for good, a consequence of which meant cutting themselves off from their family and friends (as is examined in greater detail below).

"I left him. I went to the health visitor and said I'd had enough. She arranged a refuge place, and recommended that I left the area, but I didn't really want to... my friends were here, my family's here, and (my child) was going to start school soon."

In the absence of any discussion about the violence their mothers were experiencing, and how this made them feel, some of the children who were interviewed had found it hard to understand why their mothers had not left their violent partners, or if they had left, why they had returned to them.

"... She would take us away for a week or so, but she would always go back to him.... I just couldn't understand why." (child)

One mother who was interviewed explained that she used to leave temporarily for some respite from the violence but without the clear intention of staying away for good.

"I took (my daughter) everywhere with me. I used to run with her.... I was always running with her.... I just wanted a break."

The difficulty of leaving for good

Table 8 below sets out the time which mothers spent in the violent relationship before leaving (if indeed they did).

Table 8: Time spent in the violent relationship before leaving	
duration	%
still in the relationship	23
several months	13
a year	17
2-5 years	20
6-10 years	17
11-15 years	3
more than 16 years	6
	(86 respondents)

Almost a quarter (23%) of the mothers who took part in the survey were still living in a violent relationship. Of those who had left, almost two thirds (61%) had been in the violent relationship for two years or longer, and more than a third (35%) for five years or more. The average duration of the violent relationships of women who took part in the survey was 7.3 years.

Table 9 below sets out the reasons which survey respondents gave for finding it difficult to leave their violent partner for good. It helps to explain why the mothers tended to stay in the violent relationship for some considerable time before finally deciding to leave and acting on the decision.

Table 9: Reasons mothers gave for finding it hard to leave their violent partner permanently

reason	%
afraid of what he might do	63
thought he would change	72
didn't want to end the relationship	31
too much in love with him	37
thought the violence was a "one off"	23
didn't want to leave the home	58
nowhere to go	49
couldn't afford to leave	44
family pressure not to leave	22
didn't want to upset the children	54

(102 respondents)

Emotional and material dependence

Almost three quarters (72%) of mothers said that a disincentive to leaving their violent partner for good was that they thought that he would change. More than a third (37%) said that the fact that they were so much in love had discouraged them from leaving. Less than a third (31%) said that they didn't want the relationship to end, and fewer than a quarter (23%) actually thought that the violence was an isolated incident, unlikely to recur.

These findings may be hard to understand when set against the context of sustained and severe violence apparently experienced by many of the mothers in the survey. However, it is important to remember the way in which women are often systematically disempowered by their experience of violence, especially when it is accompanied by behaviour from their partner which appears to be designed to undermine and humiliate them (as explained in the conclusion to section 2, above). Over time, living in a violent situation can have a very serious effect on women's self-confidence and on their capacity to make the decision to leave a violent partner and to act on this decision.

Several of the mothers who were interviewed also explained that they had become socially isolated as a result of living with their violent and abusive partner, thus increasing their emotional dependence on him, however unacceptable they believed his violence towards them (and sometimes their children) to be.

"I was blinded by the fact I was in love with him.... I somehow hoped that he would change and that if we got married everything would be alright."

"The trouble is that most of the time you actually do love the man, and you want to change him and make him love you like he loved you before, and no-one would ever love me so much, and I really wanted to have that thing back."

"I felt so trapped and so lonely, and I thought, 'Well, this man's the only person I've got in my whole life apart from my baby'."

Some of the violent men were also skilful at manipulating the mothers into staying or returning. One woman described, for example, how her partner had threatened that if she left she would lose the children, who were in his name; and another woman's partner had persuaded her to return on the (false) pretext that her mother was very ill.

It is also important to remember that most of the mothers in the survey were very young with young children. They had few resources of their own to fall back on and probably very poor employment prospects and earning potential – even in the unlikely event that they were able to secure affordable childcare so that they were able to go out to work. The prospect of single parenthood in such circumstances was hardly an attractive option. It is, therefore, not surprising that more than two fifths (42%) of the mothers said that they could not financially afford to leave their violent partner.

Fear of retribution

Almost two thirds (63%) of mothers said that they had been discouraged from leaving their violent partner for good by fear of what he might do to them if they did. Those women who had tried to terminate the relationship before, only for their violent partner to force his way back into the home, had particular cause to be frightened, but, as has already been observed, many of the women in the survey had experience of threats of violence being acted upon.

"It is very easy for people to say 'kick him out', but when you are that afraid of someone.... I mean I was literally terrified of this man, people just don't understand that.... Twelve years ago, if anybody had said I was going to end up a battered wife, I would have laughed at them."

"I think I probably would have left him sooner if I'd... known that I was going to be better protected by the police... if I thought that there was no chance in hell that he was going to come and attack me... But this

*fear of knowing that I was going to have to go down town on my own,
or that he might even come to my house or break a window.... and get
in.... really terrified me."*

One woman who was interviewed had previous experience of retribution
from her partner when she returned home after leaving temporarily
without her children. This was a further disincentive for her to try to
leave again.

*"Although I wanted desperately to go back to my children, I didn't want
to get back to what I knew I was going to get which would be a hiding."*

Nowhere to go and family pressures

Almost half (49%) of the mothers said that they were discouraged from
leaving permanently by the fact that they had nowhere else to go; and
more than a fifth (22%) said that they had been pressured to stay in the
relationship by their family.

One of the mothers who was interviewed explained that she felt both
these pressures acutely.

*"I did not feel there was anywhere I could go....I was under a lot of
pressure from my parents....'We can't have the shame of you going to a
battered wives refuge', which was stupid, but.... you had him on one side
and them on the other, saying, 'You can't do this, you have got to do
this...' I just felt I had nowhere to go, I had no one to talk to about it....
If there had been someone who had been through it I could have spoken
to, I might have got out years ago."*

Another mother who was interviewed had left her partner before and
stayed in a refuge. She had then gone back and felt that she couldn't go
to the refuge again because she 'felt a bit of a fraud'. (In fact, refuges
never 'judge' women in this way and will always try to accommodate
any woman seeking sanctuary, provided, of course, that they have any
free space.)

A third mother who was interviewed had left to stay with her parents in
another part of the country, but her father refused to let her stay, insisting
that she return to her partner, which she then did.

It must, therefore, have been clear to many of the mothers that in order
to escape from their partners permanently, they would need to move to
an entirely different area and 'start again' – an enormous undertaking
for a young woman with young children and few resources, worn down,
perhaps, by a considerable period of sustained abuse from her partner.

All these factors help to explain why some women apparently fantasised about leaving for good long before they felt able to act on their plans and go.

"Its hard just to take that first step and actually leave. I mean I planned for ages and ages, but I didn't think I'd ever do it."

Staying for the sake of the children

More than half (54%) of the mothers in the survey said that they were reluctant to leave their violent partner for good because they thought this would upset their children.

Several of the mothers who were interviewed mentioned that they would feel guilty about depriving their children of a father figure if they left.

"I wish I had left before my son was born, but I had this guilt that I didn't want to deprive him of a father."

However, in practice, such was the poor quality of life being endured by most of the children and their mothers at home that the children would almost certainly have been better off away. Indeed, some of the children who were interviewed commented.

"She should have gone a lot sooner.... I remember saying, 'Please, lets just go'." (child)

"She should have walked out after it (first) happened... she should have walked out (then), but she didn't." (child)

However, mothers who leave their violent partners to make a new life on their own often face considerable problems, both emotional and material, and some of these can impact on their children (as is further described below in this section).

Factors motivating mothers finally to leave their violent partners

More than four fifths (87% - 65 out of 75) of the mothers said that they had finally decided to leave their violent partners because of a "last straw". The deciding factors for these women are set out below in Table 10.

Table 10: factors which persuaded mothers finally to leave their violent partners

factors	%
realised that he would never change	86
afraid that he might kill her	68
worried about the effect on the children of witnessing the violence	66
afraid that the children would be taken into care	49
he began hitting the children	23
he threatened to harm the children	15

(65 respondents)

Almost nine tenths (86%) of the mothers for whom there had been a 'last straw' said that they had finally decided to leave because they realised that their violent partner was not going to change. More than two thirds (68%) said that the deciding factor was fear that the violence might escalate so that he would eventually kill them.

Two thirds (66%) of the mothers said that they had finally decided to leave because of their concerns about the impact on their children of witnessing the violence at home. Almost a quarter (23%) said that they decided to go when he began to hit the children; and one in six (15%) said that the final straw was when he threatened to harm the children.

Several of the mothers who were interviewed gave examples of how their violent partner's actions towards their children had prompted them to decide once and for all to leave.

"The only reason I was able to leave... at the end of the day, I would put up with everything and anything, but on this occasion he went and hit my son for no fault of his, and this is when I got the nerve, and I suppose a bit of power that.... must have been left in me, that he's not going to touch my kid.... I wasn't prepared to take that.... Until he touched the nipper I would have stuck it, I think."

"I was sitting cuddling (my daughter)... I was too frightened to let him hold her, and he started ranting and raving, and he got his roll up cigarette and he put it on (her) neck, and she was a baby, so I got up, walked out of the front door and left him."

"What actually happened in the end for me to leave my second husband was that he assaulted my youngest son... he'd wet himself, so he threw him against the toilet bowl and bruised him badly....."

Two of the mothers explained that they decided to leave because of their concern for what they believed was likely to happen to their children as a result of the violence.

"(My daughter) was just sitting there trembling and crying and stuff... I was really worried by that because I thought... its not going to be me next time, its going to be her."

"The twins were the trigger. I don't know what it was, but as soon as the twins were born I thought, 'That's it, he's out!'....I know it sounds strange because I'd had girls, but I didn't want my son growing up like his father... I didn't want him to see that."

Almost half (49%) of the women who took part in the survey said that they were concerned that unless they left, their children would be taken into care. In this context it should be remembered that one in twenty (5%) of the mothers in the survey had children who were being accommodated by the local authority as a direct result of the violence at home.

It is notable that almost three quarters (74%) of the respondents who had finally left their violent partners because of a "last straw" did so for reasons connected both to their attitude to their partner (the first two factors in the table) and to various concerns about their children (the final four factors in the table).

Leaving with the children

More than nine in ten (96% - 74 of 77 respondents) of the mothers in the survey who had left their violent partner had taken their children with them when they had done so.

Two of the mothers who were interviewed gave detailed descriptions of what had been entailed when they left their violent partners for good taking their children with them. These provide a valuable insight into how brave mothers have to be to act on a decision to leave.

"I walked out with the boy's teddy bear.... I managed to go upstairs, I got the boy's bag of cars... it was just time for the bigger one to be coming out of school so I stopped there, picked him up....'Where are we going Mum?', 'Going to see Nanny.'...He didn't quibble.... he didn't want nothing from the house, so I presume it must have been as urgent for him as it was for me.... I gets onto the railway station and I'm thinking' 'God, what are you doing here, girl? You've got no money, no nothing'.... So there's me and the nipper... on the railway station, I'm just sat there with what I've got on... my coat was over the boy, his head on his teddy

bear, and he was clutching hold of his cars."

"I did a moonlight flit. I had to wait while he were out... what I did the week before was I sneaked things out in black sacks.... because there was no way he would have let me go.... It was about 12 o'clock... they were all in bed, though they didn't know... oh no, I couldn't tell them... we just got them out of bed. My son said, 'Where are we all going?'. I said, 'You'll find out'. I just told them to get ready, hurry up and don't ask questions kind of thing... they were frightened because they all knew what he was like."

The difficulty mothers and children faced in finding somewhere to go when they left violent situations

Table 11 sets out the places where mothers in the survey said that they went after leaving their violent partner.

Table 11: Where mothers went when they left	
places	%
relatives	52
friends' homes	32
women's refuges	30
temporary housing	7
homeless	4

(90 respondents)

More than half (52%) of the women stayed with relatives; just under a third (32%) went to friends' homes, and slightly fewer (30%) to women's refuges .

One of the mothers who was interviewed explained how difficult it was in practice to stay with a friend when she first left.

"(My friend) slept on a bed settee. Her kids had her room, and I had her bed with my two. We slept in a double bed."

Two of the children who were interviewed remembered the confusion and upset of leaving home.

"I had to go and stay with my auntie for two weeks. My mother and brother were in a battered wives' place... they were staying over there in a safe house sort of thing." (child)

"My mother just grabbed our stuff, and she took me down there, and then I didn't see her till the next day. And she was over at that refuge for about two weeks" (child)

The disruption caused to the lives of mothers and their children when they leave violent relationships

Table 12 sets out the changes which mothers in the survey said they had to make after having left their violent partners for good.

Table 12: Changes made after having left the violent partner for good	
changes	%
new friends for self	78
new friends for children	61
children's school	48
nursery/playgroup	37
doctor (GP)	61
social worker	28
health visitor	39
(46 respondents)	

Table 12 shows how extremely disturbing it is to mothers' - and especially to childrens' - lives to leave a violent relationship and to have to start afresh.

More than three quarters (78%) of the mothers who answered this question said that they had to find new friends for themselves after they left their violent partner for good. This may have been for a number of reasons: for example, because without the relationship with their partner they needed to form new relationships, or because the breach with him meant that the mothers lost their 'joint' friends, or because leaving permanently entailed leaving the area and starting a completely new life elsewhere.

Quite clearly, when mothers and children leave a violent partner, the children often experience very considerable changes to their lives. Almost two thirds (61%) of children had to find new friends, and almost half (48%) had to change schools. This may have been because they had moved to a new school catchment area or from fear that the violent partner would trace mother and child via the child's original school.

This means that many children whose mothers leave violent relationships face the loss of their homes (and possibly many of their possessions if their mothers have to leave very quickly), their schools and their friends. The children will also often have to adjust to a relationship with their father which is going to be quite different (if indeed it continues to exist at all, as is explained below), and all this at a time when the children and their mothers may be extremely upset by the events which have led them to leave in the first place. The extent of these changes is such that it may help to explain why so many children appear to be profoundly affected in the short and the longer term by their experience of domestic violence.

Almost two thirds (61%) of women had also changed their doctor, probably because they had moved beyond their GP's catchment area. This change may have been quite disruptive and upsetting for many of the mothers, especially for those who had become reliant on their GPs for medical advice and general support for themselves and their children and who used their surgery as an access point for other health care services.

How the children felt about having left

Table 13 sets out how mothers in the survey believed their children reacted to having left home and the violent partner (who was often the children's father).

Table 13: Mothers' views of their children's reactions to having left home and the violent partner

Children's reactions	%
Didn't understand the need to leave	41
Missed their father	41
Felt safer	33
Were relieved	28
Upset about leaving belongings	25
Upset about leaving school and friends	20

(61 respondents)

Table 13 demonstrates how mixed children's reactions often are to the experience of leaving home and their mother's violent partner. More than two fifths (41%) of mothers thought that their children didn't understand why they had left, and the same proportion thought that their children missed their father. A third (33%) of mothers thought their children felt safer, and slightly fewer (28%) thought that the children were relieved to be away. A quarter (25%) thought that the children were upset at leaving behind their possessions (which might of course, include pets), and a fifth (20%) thought they were distressed at leaving their school and their friends.

As one of the children who was interviewed commented, confusion at the scale of the changes they had to endure may often be the dominant reaction, especially initially and for young children.

"At the time, I felt confused more than anything. I was frightened. I didn't know what was happening." (child)

The difficulties children (and their mothers) encounter in re-negotiating the relationship with their father after having left

Comments made by some of the mothers and children who were interviewed demonstrate some of the difficulties encountered by children and their mothers in re-negotiating the relationship with their fathers after their mothers had left.

Two of the children who were interviewed explained that their mothers' violent partners had known where they lived after they had left and continued to be a threat to them for some considerable time.

"He pestered us for a long time after that. Nobody could come near us. He'd be waiting all the time... we couldn't have visitors or anything." (child)

"I was about eleven or twelve when they split up... but we still had hassle off him for a couple of years, like. He would come up to the house and try and push his way in. He would kick the door down." (child)

Problems for the mothers often continued when their violent partners maintained some kind of contact with their children after they had left. Of course, there are often difficulties between parents concerning access arrangements, but when there has been a history of violence in the relationship, these are greatly magnified, especially for mothers.

Two mothers who were interviewed explained how traumatic and confusing they felt that access had been for their sons.

"The whole year after we split up... a whole year of mixed feelings... he'd stop at the weekends with his Dad, and he'd come back and he'd hate me. He'd want to kick me and he scratched me... it took me about an hour to calm him down... After about a year it stopped, and he said, 'Oh, I'm fed up with my Daddy, my Daddy lets me down... he doesn't keep his promises. You don't break your promises Mummy, you're always there.' he said, 'But I do love my Daddy'... and that's when all the problems at school started... the confusion coming in."

"Even now there have still been arguments on the doorstep when his Dad comes to collect him... I think he anticipates the aggression.... I think that its confusing for (my son). He obviously wants to think the best of me and of his Dad, but with his father saying things.... he actually said to (my son) to say that I was a silly cow."

Several of the mothers gave examples of ways in which their violent partners used their children to try to 'get back' at them after they had left.

"He tried pinching (my daughter) a few times when she was younger... taking her from me, locking himself in his mother's.... just to get at me, it was you know, to get me going and start the police going, because he used to like it when I called the police... he thought it was great to have a fight."

"My husband tried to get custody of the children.... I don't think he wanted them, but I don't think he wanted me to have them, either."

"He would put her into care. He would have her adopted. And I was just so afraid of him that I really thought he would do it."

"I'm worried about them being hurt... he's talking about how I'm not going to have them for much longer, and the only way that he will get them is illegally... if he was to take them, the perfect opportunity was when he had them for the weekend, so this is a constant anxiety."

Two other mothers remarked on how difficult they found any contact with their violent ex-partner now that they had left.

"He turns up out of the blue, usually when he knows my boyfriend is out... he's usually been drinking... and I'm scared even to sit in the same room as him now."

"I lose my temper quite quickly... especially if I know he's coming that day to pick (the children) up. I really hate the thought of actually seeing him... I look forward to those weekends when they go away, even though I miss them, but I worry about them."

Another mother was quite determined that her children should keep in touch with their father, however difficult this was for her and however unreliable he was.

"My son don't understand because he's only five and the presents I bought, I put from Mum and Dad, because I wouldn't hurt the children... they've got to know their father."

Discussion: leaving a violent partner is tremendously hard to do

The study findings discussed here, both quantitative and qualitative, help to explain why mothers find it so very difficult to leave their violent partners once and for all. Indeed, such were the difficulties of leaving for many of the women in the study that it is rather remarkable that more than three quarters of them (77%) had in fact managed to leave the violent relationship at all.

One of the important conclusions suggested by the findings reported in this section is that the "choices" facing many mothers who are thinking of leaving are in fact far less attractive than one might otherwise suppose. In deciding whether or not to leave, most of the mothers in this study had to weigh up many competing considerations. In particular, the actual process of trying to leave for good was likely to be fraught with problems - for example, their violent partners might find out and take out their anger on the mothers or their children.

Moreover, the final outcome was equally clouded with uncertainty. Would she ever be safe from him, or would he succeed in tracking them down, however far away they went - as he had always said? To have any chance of escaping from him, wouldn't she have to cut herself off completely from her present life, leaving her home and severing all ties with family and friends? And the children would probably have to change schools and make new friends. Would they blame her for disrupting their lives? Would they be better off if they stayed or if they went? How would she manage to support them all and bring up the children on her own, if she did leave? Where would they all live? These are just a few of the many questions mothers contemplating leaving their violent partners usually had to consider.

It is important to bear in mind that most mothers in the study, faced with trying to decide the best thing to do in this situation, were very young, with small children. They had little money and poor employment prospects They were also relatively isolated and probably worn down by a period of sustained violence and abuse. It is, therefore, little wonder that so many who had left had taken a relatively long time before finally deciding to leave and feeling able to act on their plans.

One mother expressed particularly well how hard it is to find the strength to leave, but how good it feels, especially in terms of regaining some control over your life, if you can do so.

"The doctor gave me anti-depressants after (my son) was born... the good thing was, though, that I actually got better, and when I was better I asked (my violent partner) to leave, and that's when everything fell into place... After a few months it started to lift... I knew what the right thing was to do... I knew what I wanted for my son and myself and I did something about it...."

Clearly, despite all the problems that mothers and children face when they leave a violent situation, there are also enormous compensations. One mother, whose partner's behaviour had been particularly sadistic, said very simply:

"Now we are more like normal people, doing normal things that normal families do."

And one of the children who was interviewed commented:

"I was so happy when my Mum and him split up." (child)

9. How domestic violence can become a 'shared family secret'

Two thirds (66% – 65 of 99) of mothers in the survey said that they had felt unable to tell anyone about the violence when it first happened. The time which they said did elapse before telling someone else about their experience of domestic violence is set out in Table 14 below.

The difficulty of telling others about the violence

Table 14: The time which elapsed before mothers spoke about the violence

Time before telling	%
Not told anyone yet	3
several months	35
a year	12
2-5 years	19
6-10 years	6
11-15 years	1
more than 15 years	3

(65 respondents)

The average time taken to tell someone, excluding those who had not yet told anyone, was between one and two years. Survey respondents gave a wide range of reasons for being unable to tell anyone about the violence, including the following: "*I thought he would change*"; "*I was too embarrassed*"; "*I was ashamed*"; "*I was too scared*"; "*I felt it was my fault*"; "*no one would have believed me*"; "*we were living with his family*"; "*I had no friends left I could tell*".

Some of the mothers who were interviewed said that they had no need to tell anyone – various people already knew, or had guessed. In some cases they were supportive.

"People could see, despite my attempts to hide the injuries... they'd say, 'Get rid of him'."

In other cases, they were less helpful.

"The family knew what was going on.... but it was only when he died that they were all terribly concerned about me and the children – which really angered me for a long time."

Comments from some of the mothers who were interviewed showed that families are not always as supportive of women who are experiencing violence as might be expected. Some spoke of being strongly encouraged to stay in the violent situation by their parents. There were a number of reasons for this: fear of embarrassment if they left, concern at possible trouble with other relatives, or for the sake of the children. These views tended to reinforce the doubts that some women already had about the wisdom of leaving and fed into their own feelings of guilt and shame.

Barriers to seeking professional help

More than two thirds (70% - 58 of 83) of mothers who took part in the survey said that they had found it difficult to tell professionals about problems their children might be having because of the violence at home. The reasons they gave for this are set out in Table 15 below.

Table 15: Reasons given for finding it hard to seek professional help for the children

reason	%
felt guilty	81
afraid the children would be taken away	74
didn't know who to tell	43
thought the children would be alright	12

(58 respondents)

More than four fifths (81%) of mothers gave 'feeling guilty' as a reason for finding it difficult to seek professional help for their children; and almost three quarters (74%) had been frightened that if they spoke honestly to professionals that their children might be taken away. More than two fifths (43%) said that they didn't know who to tell. Only one in eight (12%) of the mothers had been deterred from seeking out professional help for their children by the belief that they and their children were managing on their own.

Several of the mothers who were interviewed spoke of their own, and other women's, fear that their children would be removed by Social Services if they disclosed to them the true nature of the violence they had experienced at home.

"Social services was helpful, but I always had that thing in the back of my mind that they'd take away (my child), and that would have been it."

"... Lots of Mums come to see me, some that are being abused by their husbands, they come to see me because they daren't tell anybody else... they're frightened their children will be removed."

"She got taken off me several times with Social Services. Obviously, I got her back the next day, or I went to a women's refuge with her.... we travelled all over the place, me and her, and I wouldn't want to see the other two go through that."

Women and children concealing the violence

Some of the mothers and children who were interviewed gave examples of ways in which they had managed to keep the truth about what was going on at home from others, not least out of concern that the children might be removed from the family and/or the mother might be blamed.

"I was frightened of what other people might say and the stigma attached with your mother.... whether they think your own mother is battering you and your brother or whatever. I didn't want people to think that because it wasn't true. I didn't want people to take pity on me." (child)

"My teacher tried to find out, but I just didn't let anything slip. I just said, 'No, everything's okay.' You just smile, don't you, and try to cover it like.... I don't think I wanted anyone to know, because I was embarrassed that it was going on, so I tried to cover it up." (child)

"I was frightened of telling anyone... it would have been worse because I wasn't sixteen and.... perhaps they would have taken me into homes..." (child)

"You hear so many things about social workers...." (child)

Some of the mothers and children said that they could not speak out from fear that the violent partner would find out and punish them.

"A child ain't going to tell you everything while they're still in a situation for fear of being beaten up because of it." (child)

".... At the age I am now I think, well, I can't really say nothing. Its like I know this interview is confidential, but I can't really say nothing, just in case they go back out and say something, and it gets round to my Dad... he opens all our mail, and he'd read it and he'd hit me.... I'd get done for saying something." (child)

"I never had enough courage to go (and tell anyone)." (child)

"I was too frightened (to get help) really...He'll say, 'Where are you going, what are you doing?' and how can I say, 'Well, I'm trying to talk to someone about this relationship'?"

Several of the mothers who were interviewed explained how they had 'kept officialdom at bay' from fear that their children would be removed. One said that she had not attended ante-natal classes because of the bruises. Another had provided her daughter's nursery with an excuse for her child's obvious distress.

"I didn't actually want to give the full story of what had been behind it, so I said, 'Well, I've just left her father so maybe she's feeling a little bit insecure'. and I said just to keep an eye on her."

A third woman had learnt from experience that it was better not to tell the Social Services what was happening at home.

"In the end (the Social Services) got fed up. They explained to me that any more and I'd have (my daughter) taken off me, so every time he'd start I'd just up and go to my mother's.... but I thought, 'I can't go to the Social Services, they're not taking my baby off me for the likes of him'... I didn't go to them for help after that.... they used to phone and ask how things were... I used to say okay, just to keep the peace... but I used to worry, 'Oh, they're not taking her'."

Discussion: Unless mothers and children decide to tell about the violence at home, it may often continue undetected

The study findings reported in this section show how difficult it is for mothers and children to tell other people about their experiences of domestic violence; fear of retribution from the violent partner, fear that the interventions of social workers will make things worse, not better. These and a sense of shame are powerful disincentives. Moreover, domestic violence is such an intrinsically personal matter that, as one mother who was interviewed commented:

"No-one to this day I have ever spoken to really knows the full extent of what happened to me in that relationship and there's still some things that you won't talk about and you can't. It's like they remain locked up, sort of, there, and nobody will ever know, and I don't think that any woman that is abused will ever tell the full story."

It seems that many of the mothers and children in the study had colluded quite successfully to prevent outsiders from knowing what was really happening to them at home. In this way, domestic violence can become a shared family secret, certainly not discussed 'outside' – and perhaps not even talked about openly or acknowledged at home.

However, both the survey and interview data from the study show that it would be quite wrong to conclude from the reticence of mothers and children that they found the violence in any way acceptable. Both women and children seemed very clear that the violence and abuse they were experiencing were intolerable - the difficulty lay in finding a way to improve their situation.

As is discussed further in the next section, it is understandable that the statutory services become frustrated if they are repeatedly called out by mothers experiencing domestic violence only for these women apparently, to 'choose' to remain with their violent partners – even though these study findings show how difficult it is for mothers to leave their violent partners for good. However, it is clear that if social services for example, suggest to any mother that if they are alerted again the mother's child may be removed, all this is likely to achieve is to 'scare her off' from contacting them ever again. This does not help to safeguard the mother or her child.

This consideration, together with the secrecy that often seems to surround domestic violence, suggest that any measures drawn up to help mothers and children who are suffering from domestic violence must be designed to be perceived as genuinely supportive and not punitive; otherwise sufferers from domestic violence will simply be driven 'further underground'.

10. Mothers' experiences of the helpfulness of statutory services

Table 16 sets out the answers mothers gave to the question of whether or not they had found certain statutory services to be helpful in the context of the domestic violence they had experienced.

Table 16: The helpfulness of statutory services

Service	Unhelpful %	Helpful %
Police	32	45
Social services	15	36
Doctor (GP)	16	25

(85 respondents)

The Police

More mothers had found the police to be helpful (45%) than unhelpful (32%).

Some of the mothers who were interviewed, however, gave examples of incidents in which they felt that they had been let down by the police. In fact, while some of the incidents they described certainly reveal a lack of sensitivity and understanding on the part of police officers, others suggest that some violent men are as adept at keeping away the police as some mothers and children are at 'fending off' the 'caring professions'.

Some of the women's frustrations were generated not so much by police action (or lack of it), but by their experience of the criminal court system's tendency to deal leniently with men who are violent towards women. They found that 'the system' is often ineffective in protecting women and children from men determined to be violent.

"(I called the police).... He was kicking the door down. I was inside. The kids were outside with him... the police said that there was nothing they could do as I didn't have an injunction. The kids told me that he was taken away in a police car, and they were left on the doorstep."

"(My violent partner) said to his brother, 'Just tell (the police) it was a domestic argument and that everything's okay'. So there's me, gushing blood, all my eye, all my shoulder black, oh, I was in a hell of a state and the police came round to the back of the house and I was sniffling, so I thought they would hear me.... He was like smothering me in the chair... The police said to his brother, 'If that girl needs hospital treatment, you're to blame.' obviously for not letting them in... he just said to the police that it had all quietened down... 'she's okay.'... the police called (my partner) a psychopath, that's what he was known as at the police station." (This woman took out a number of injunctions against her partner, but found that they did not protect her from his violence.)

"(My violent partner) was sitting across the front door with this machete. (The police officer) said, 'Jump across.' I said, 'I can't because he'll cut my legs or something with it.'..... lucky enough... I jumped across him and he whacks right across the policeman's knees... he had stitches... but the things (my violent partner) has done and got away with.... he's never been to prison... its unbelievable."

One mother who was interviewed had been raped by her violent partner. She called the police and was taken to the rape unit.

"(Several hours later)... I had changed my mind about taking him to court... It's quite a scary thing to do... all I can remember him saying was that I'd had wasted police time, because, you know, I suppose I'd called the police several times before that in the course of the previous months... I don't think they really realise just how difficult it is for women in that position to go through with taking someone to court.... How would I explain to my children where their father was?... It would be a terrible stigma for them and I don't want them to have to put up with that... it would be as if he was punishing us even by doing that... and if he went to prison that wouldn't change him, and when he came out he'd probably be so angry that he'd come after us."

Another mother who was interviewed felt very strongly that the police should always alert the social services when called to a domestic violence incident where children were involved.

"...I really do feel.... if police is called to a domestic violence incident, that they should be put straight onto social services.... otherwise things go on for years.... undetected, and then that's years that children are in them homes and watching their mothers get knocked from pillar to post, like my girls were."

The social services

More mothers had found social services to be helpful (36%) than unhelpful (15%). This is encouraging given the wariness towards social workers expressed by many of the mothers and children (as described above).

Two of the mothers who were interviewed, however, had been disappointed not to receive more help from social services.

"(I had to ask for help).... I suppose I couldn't understand why we hadn't been allocated a social worker... the court case was over and... you know, that was it."

Another mother felt that the social services had failed to offer her any constructive help with her fears of what might be happening to her children during access visits to their father, given that she believed that he used to leave them on their own and go out drinking. *"All they said was, 'You can go to a refuge'."*

Finally, one child who was interviewed said that she had told a social worker about the violence at home but hadn't been believed.

Doctors

More respondents had found doctors to be helpful (25%) than unhelpful (16%).

However, once again, several of the mothers interviewed had been disappointed that their doctor had not been of greater help. One mother tried to speak to her GP about her concerns for her eight year old daughter. She said *"I don't think the doctor really understood it.... there wasn't time in a normal appointment to get it across."*

Another woman described how, after her husband had hurt her leg, he wouldn't let her out: *"Because he knew he'd done something to my leg and I couldn't walk on it... I made an excuse that I needed to go to the doctor for some more pills... but (once there) I burst into tears. It all blurted out and he looked at my leg... he said 'rest'...he gave me some painkillers, and he gave me some more pills, even though I didn't need them.... he followed this up with a home visit with the health visitor.... they kept telling me I should leave him, but I said, 'I'm frightened to... he's going to kill me if I leave'."*

Schools

Mothers taking part in the survey were not asked about their experiences of the helpfulness or otherwise of their children's schools, but several who were interviewed commented about this.

One mother had found her children's school very helpful at a practical level, making arrangements to minimise the risk of her husband abducting her sons after she had left him. However, they never offered to talk about the issue with her. (Although it is not clear whether she had ever asked for this help).

Another mother had tried to discuss the problems at home at her child's school, but: *"they said, well, they never had any problems with her, and I said, 'No, well, its not that sort of problem.'...."*

Discussion: Mothers and children sometimes do not know where to turn, and what help the statutory sector presently provides could be made more effective and coherent

It is encouraging that more mothers had found the statutory services to be helpful than unhelpful, but comments made by those who were interviewed suggest that some women do not know where to find help.

"I was just left to get on, you know... I had no help from... anyone. There was no advice, there was nobody to go to, there was no social worker, no nothing..."

"... I don't know where to turn really...."

Some local authorities have taken steps to help fill this information gap by reaching out to women who are suffering domestic violence. Islington Borough Council, for example, has published a booklet explaining where women can obtain confidential help and providing general advice and reassurance. Such initiatives should become standard practice in all local authorities.

The study also demonstrates how women become frustrated with the style and timing of statutory sector interventions. Yet police officers, courts and social workers sometimes feel hampered in trying to help mothers by their apparent 'unwillingness' to leave their violent partner, to move to a different area or to take legal action against him. There are other frustrations about the difficulty of enforcing injunctions against men who are determined to be violent. This can make the women concerned terrified and afraid to act.

Some of these problems may be intrinsic to 'domestic violence', in that so much of the violence and abuse, and the fear this engenders, is connected to the power and control which the men in these relationships seem to wield over women. It is, therefore, difficult for outsiders to intervene effectively in these situations, even if they are backed up by the full force of the law.

However, it is clear that statutory interventions to help mothers and children living in violent situations could often be much more strategic and determined than at present. Part of the power which men wield over mothers and children living in violent relationships lies in their shared knowledge that if the woman leaves, she faces a very uncertain future in terms of housing, income and protection from him. This unequal power relationship, which often enables violent men to 'keep hold' of mothers and children, despite the fact that the violence has long since become intolerable to them, would be significantly altered if three simple policy changes were implemented in favour of all mothers and children leaving violent situations:

i)   speedy access to decent, permanent, affordable accommodation;
ii)   automatic entitlement to adequate welfare benefits, and, in time, the ability to access good quality training and child care, so enabling these mothers to work to support themselves and their children;
iii) a right to determined police protection (including, for example,

the installation of panic buttons at home which would immediately alert the police) should their violent partners try to attack them.

If changes of this nature were introduced, the ability of the statutory services to help mothers and children living in violent situations would be greatly enhanced.

11. The support that mothers and children believe is wanted

Slightly more than half of mothers (54% - 42 of 78) said that they thought their children could have been better helped to deal with their experiences of domestic violence. Table 17 below sets out the services and help which these women would have liked their children to have received.

Table 17: The help needed by children experiencing domestic violence

type of help	%
counselling for the children	71
learning about domestic violence at school	64
someone for the children to talk to	57
somewhere safe for the children to go	43

(42 respondents)

Almost three quarters (71%) of the mothers thought their children would have benefitted from counselling; almost two thirds (64%) would have liked their children to have learnt about domestic violence at school; more than half (57%) would have liked their children to have had someone to talk to; and more than two fifths (43%) would have liked there to have been somewhere safe for their children to go.

Help for children

Most of the mothers and children interviewed spoke of the importance of providing support for children who were experiencing, and who had experienced, domestic violence.

"It would probably have helped to have more counselling. It would help the children.... I've experienced with (my son) the anger and the upset.... he feels that a lot of it is his fault. And I think that children in these situations could do with more sort of help.... because sometimes.... it's hard to talk to him....You don't want to bias him, to let him know how much you hate his father, and so another person, a more neutral person, (would be better)."

"I didn't know how the children were feeling inside about things.... maybe they would open up to someone else."

Most of the children interviewed said they thought they would have benefitted from having had someone to talked to about the violence. This would have helped them to understand what had happened and to break their sense of isolation.

"I didn't get any support, so I bottled things up. It would have been good to have talked about it." (child)

"You have people with, like, mental and physical violence in the home and people too often just forget what the effects of that are on the child, you know. Whether they see it, or hear it, or see the after-effects of the bruises and everything.... they never explain to you how it happened or anything, you just don't know anything." (child)

"They could have a break from the violence... so they could have some pleasure... I got to the stage I just didn't care... I always used to be so unhappy, you know, all on my own." (child)

"Activities would have helped at the time, I suppose, to take my mind off it, going out more often, not being in the house so much, definitely. Because then maybe Mum and him might have appreciated us more... we wouldn't have been around them so much, getting in the way.... it would've given them a break as well to sort out their problems." (child)

"If there'd been children here, you could make friends, couldn't you? And understand that you're not alone, so maybe you would talk about it." (child)

"Everything was focussed on my mother, you know, like how was my mother, was she going back to him or was she going to build her own life. But to us, it was just, 'Are you okay?', and you would say yes out of politeness. And that was it.... you don't understand at that age." (child)

One child who was interviewed said that she felt that it would take some time before a child living in a violent situation would feel able to talk about what had happened.

"Because its like a stranger, and you wouldn't go up to a stranger in the street and tell them your problems, which is what a social worker is in a way. You don't know them. I think before a child would talk about it, he would have to build a bond with them, because I wouldn't have gone out and talked to anybody about it." (child)

Help for mothers

Some of the mothers who were interviewed expressed strong views about the type of support they would have liked and when they would have most valued it. Counselling and advice were services several mothers mentioned as being helpful.

"(When you leave) you need someone to talk to and say, 'Well, why did I do this and why did I put up with it for this long, and what did I put my child through?'....there's so many questions but there's nobody there answering them."

"You don't want to be told... to leave him... you don't want to be told how stupid you are. You want somebody that will listen to it, and maybe advise or whatever or talk about the children and the effects, the short and long term effects it can have, to make you aware and make you wake up to what's going on, and not somebody that's going to sit there and judge."

Several mothers emphasised that there was a need in their own cases for help to rebuild their relationships with their children - to learn how to talk to them again, especially about the violence and how they felt about it. (A previous section has already examined how few mothers discuss the violence with their children and the problems this can produce for the children). To this end, they felt that counselling for themselves and their children together would be very useful.

"I've always felt okay talking to them about pills, and, I mean, the little one's talked to me about AIDs, you know. I don't have a problem.... but as far as my own experience of abuse, I find it very difficult."

"I would have sought help a long time before I actually did and both my boys and myself are now having...help to bond....to build up the relationship between ourselves so that we can talk to each other, because I haven't been able to talk to my children either."

"(Counselling as a family unit) would have given us much more confidence to face the future....."

"I needed help to learn how to talk to the children.... I didn't know how. I thought I might do more damage by putting it back again....I needed that help earlier. Now it is almost too late because I have buried it and blocked it out... I don't want to raise the hurt again."

Informal support networks can be a lifeline

Both the mothers and children who were interviewed testified to the vital role informal support can play in helping those who are experiencing domestic violence.

Two of the children in particular felt that this had done more than anything else to keep them going.

"I saw my grandparents quite a lot... if it wasn't for them I wouldn't have got through it, I don't think.... They just took me away from it all.... I didn't tell them the whole story. It was a feeling of being loved you know.... my grandfather made me feel worth something.... and I also had loads of friends.... that's how I got by." (child)

"I could tell (my friend) how I felt and stuff... but, on occasions, when he used to do some really awful stuff, like, I thought, 'Oh, shall I tell her...what would she think of me?' But I always used to tell her at the end of the day.... because she was my crying on my shoulder friend. But I did find it a relief because I couldn't tell my mother, because it was all her problem..... at the time you think its your fault.... I was always afraid (my friend) would think less of me because of what my father was like.... and I lived in her house practically all the time. I would do anything to stay away." (child)

And one of the mothers who was interviewed stressed how useful self-help groups could be.

"I think, yes... (help has to come) from experienced people, say social workers.... but also to have a team of mothers.... people who have actually been through it.... They find it much easier to talk to you about it...."

12. The role of family centres
· ·

A question in the survey asked mothers whether or not the NCH Action For Children Family Centre with which they were in contact had been helpful to them with respect to their experience of domestic violence. Just over half of the respondents (53% - 40 of 76) said that it had. Table 18 below describes the ways in which these mothers felt that their family centre had helped.

Ways in which family centres can help

Table 18: Ways in which NCH Action For Children family centres had helped mothers and children experiencing domestic violence

service	%
counselling for respondent	90
play facilities for children	88
child care for respite	53
help with benefits, housing etc.	40
women's support group	40
counselling for children	38

(40 respondents)

Nine in ten (90%) of the mothers who had been helped had received counselling for themselves; almost the same proportion (88%) had benefitted from the provision of play facilities for their children. More than half (53%) had been able to have respite child care; and two fifths (40%) had joined a women's support (self-help) group. Two fifths (40%) had also received help with claiming benefits and with accessing housing. The children of slightly less than two fifths (38%) had received counselling at the project.

Some of the mothers and children interviewed explained what they found particularly valuable about the services they were receiving.

"(The children) mainly just play, from what I can make out (they were seen separately from me...I see a counsellor).... I think they were closed up for so long and you know, not allowed to be children as such... not allowed to do so many things, that it was like catching up with all they missed out. So all this playing... is their way of coping with it."

"(Its been) somewhere for them to play... and for me to get out... since (my son's) been coming here, he's getting better.. cos' like we don't mix with nobody, kind of thing."

"I think that this place here is brilliant.... somewhere you can bring the children and visit other people, so I really can have a couple of hours peace from them, and help and support...(my son) loves it here, all the things that they do for them."

"(NCH Action For Children) gave me a wonderful social worker.... she's been really helping.... I've said to her that's she's more than welcome to talk to us all... at any time, because I just feel that what's needed here is a lot of healing."

"(My son) was able to talk to (the social worker).... she was wonderful, and there was nobody like her by the time she got to know him... and I'm thinking, 'Well maybe I'm missing out a little bit here!'"

One of the mothers who was interviewed had recently been involved in a court case concerning access by her partner to her child.

"(The staff at the project) just listened and backed me up really, and its been somewhere to come as well. When he's been really violent its been somewhere to run, when I've been frightened of what he might do."

Two of the mothers thought it was especially important that there were male workers at the NCH Action For Children family centres they attended. Although they initially had some reservations, they both agreed that this had helped them and their children begin to learn to trust men again after their experiences of domestic violence.

"I wasn't too sure at first, especially as he was a man... we sort of became really good friends, and he's come to visit me every week, and we sit on the settee.... chatting away like old friends... He introduced me to this place.... He said, 'Why don't you go up there... have a break for a couple of hours?'... and I thought, 'Well, I don't know, its not really my scene.'.... but I've been coming here ever since. I've joined women's groups. I've introduced friends to come here."

"...They really like (their male social worker)... I think it is much more important that they have some kind of male influence in their life....s he wouldn't run and hide in another room or anything."

One child who was interviewed summed up what she valued most in 'her' social worker.

"She doesn't talk to you as if you are a problem, she talks to you like a friend... and, like, she will come up to the house... and have a coffee and stuff like that... she treats you as a person, whereas a lot of social workers don't. They talk to you as if you're just a problem child.... She was the only person.... that I really told the full story to, and that, what used to happen and the reasons why and stuff like that." (child)

Discussion: Community based support services, such as family centres, play an important role helping women and children who experience domestic violence

It seems clear from this study that many family centres do a great deal of work to help support mothers and children who are experiencing domestic violence, even though these resources are mostly designed to work with children who are more generally in need or at risk and their families. Family centres may in fact do more work in the context of domestic violence than their staff sometimes recognise. One of their attractions for some mothers and children may be that they can use their services without having to acknowledge explicitly, at least to start with, that they are living in a violent situation.

The comments of some of the mothers about the importance they attached to having male workers in projects are interesting. Clearly, there is a need for sensitivity on the part of projects and their staffs in this respect. Not all mothers and children who are experiencing, or who have experienced, violence may feel that they wish to work with male workers. However, for these mothers and children, just seeing men in a friendly environment may help them and their children to build up trust and to recognise that not all men abuse power.

Conclusions

This study of the effects of domestic violence has been based on the contributions of more than one hundred and eight mothers and their two hundred and forty six children living in cities, towns and rural areas throughout Great Britain. The research has, therefore, by necessity, glossed over the sheer diversity of experience to be found in such a relatively large number of lives. At this point it may be important to stress again that everyone's experience of domestic violence is different, and that each case should be treated individually. (Perhaps Tolstoy was right: *"All happy families are alike but an unhappy family is unhappy after its own fashion."* – the opening words of *Anna Karenina*).

It is important to acknowledge the value of individual experience, but equally vital to examine what this study tells us about the general impact on children and their mothers of living in a violent situation. The survey and interview findings certainly provide many insights about this, the most important of which are the following.

What 'living in a violent situation' really means for children and mothers

The research shows very clearly what 'living in a violent situation' means for children and their mothers. Between a half and two thirds of mothers in the survey experienced severe and recurrent physical and/or sexual violence. The children of more than a quarter of mothers in the survey were also being physically abused by their mother's violent partner. The children of almost three quarters had seen their mothers being physically attacked by their partners.

Some of the descriptions in the research of the violence experienced by mothers and experienced or witnessed by their children are shocking, but perhaps of even greater concern is how the study shows that these eruptions of violence often occur in households in which the man's entire behaviour seems to be designed to undermine, humiliate and degrade the mother and, sometimes, also the children. In these circumstances, the violent man often comes to have complete authority within the family, particularly within the four walls of the family home.

The study also shows that these relationships are neither transient (their average length was 7.3 years, and the men were fathers to one or more children in the family in the overwhelming majority of cases) nor ones in which outbreaks of physical violence are simply accompanying the relationship's terminal decline. Systematic violence and abuse visited by men on women and sometimes children is intrinsic to how some of these relationships have come to operate. As such it becomes immediately obvious that they are of a qualitatively different nature from those more usually encountered in which men and women involved in a genuine partnership are simply 'going through a bad patch'.

Explanations for domestic violence

There is, therefore, a significant gulf between the popular image of domestic violence and the reality as it emerges from this research. For most of the women and children who took part in this study, 'living in a violent situation' meant enduring abuse which was much more sustained and systematic than merely having Dad coming home drunk on Saturday night and lashing out unsteadily at Mum before passing out (although that is bad enough). Indeed, intoxication due to drink or drugs emerges from this study, as from most previous research, as a complete 'red herring' in the search for explanations of domestic violence.

Similarly, there was absolutely no evidence whatsoever in this study to suggest that women are in any way attracted to violent relationships. The mothers who took part in the research reflected on their experiences with mixed emotions, including horror, sadness, regret, shame, guilt, and profound weariness, but pleasure on their part was never once mentioned, or even hinted at.

Instead, this study confirms beyond any doubt that the responsibility for the violence lies clearly with those who perpetrate it – the men. Were the men in this study motivated by sadism or the desire to assert complete control over their female partners and often their children? Did the family circumstances their behaviour produced give them some level of satisfaction? Questions such as these are beyond the scope of this study, but they are matters in urgent need of investigation, if we are to further our understanding of why domestic violence occurs and how it can be prevented.

The impact on children of living in a violent situation

This research contains a great deal of evidence to support the view that domestic violence has a serious adverse impact on the great majority of children who encounter it and that the effects are usually both short and longer term. Crucially, the research suggests, this is so whether the violence is experienced by children directly (through associated physical abuse) or indirectly (through witnessing the violence and its aftermath, and through living with a violent man).

Once one appreciates what living in a violent situation really means for children and their mothers, it is scarcely surprising that this should be so. The violence which many of the children had experienced was such that they were often left, years later, with extremely vivid recollections of what had happened and how they felt, even if they had been scarcely older than toddlers at the time. In this sense, the violence was a genuinely traumatic event for them. Moreover, domestic violence is the enemy of many of the features of family life which help children to grow up feeling happy and confident. Stability, trust, continuity, reciprocity and a sense of security for example, are likely to be lacking in families in which men are systematically violent and abusive.

While children are very young and/or still living in a violent situation, they seem often to react to domestic violence by becoming frightened and withdrawn or running away; or by becoming aggressive; or by 'taking sides' in the conflict; or perhaps, most typically of all, by acting in any number of apparently conflicting ways, reflecting their confusion and hurt.

This research shows that once children are no longer living in a violent situation and/or are older, the longer term effects often include a general lack of self-confidence; violent and aggressive behaviour towards other people; sadness; and a desire, perhaps especially on the part of daughters, to avoid involvement in personal relationships with men.

The consequences of these longer term effects on children's behaviour are very concerning. At best, they imply that there may be many adolescents and young adults who are unhappy and unwilling or unable to engage in close relationships with others. At worst, they suggest that bitter and resentful young people may be acting violently towards others as a direct result of their unresolved feelings about the violence they experienced as children.

The study also demonstrates the complex ways in which domestic violence can erode the relationship between mothers and children in both the short and the longer term. This is particularly damaging for these children since the relationships they have with their fathers are also likely to be difficult, if indeed they exist at all. In the absence of professional help, it seems that many mothers and children are left feeling uncomfortable with each other. The children are often resentful at 'being deprived of a childhood', as they sometimes understandably perceive it, and may lack understanding of the difficult position their mothers found themselves in. The mothers themselves are left feeling guilty and inadequate.

This research suggests that both mothers and children often feel to blame for the violence, and guilty about their reactions to it, in both the short and the longer term. In this sense it is ironic that it is the victims, rather than the perpetrators of the violence, who seem so often to take responsibility for what has happened within the family. Both mothers and children need to understand that the violence was not their fault, and professional help may be required if they are fully to accept this and learn to live together again.

In this context, it is important to understand that this study shows that domestic violence and its aftermath can force children away from home in one of two ways. Firstly, some children grow up away from their mothers – with their fathers, other relatives or in foster/residential care – as a direct result of the violence. Secondly, other young people leave home prematurely and in an unplanned way because they find the violence at home intolerable, or because it has destroyed their relationships with their mothers and/or their mothers' partners.

In these ways, domestic violence is likely to have a seriously adverse impact on the long term life chances of these children, particularly those who grow up in care or who leave home prematurely since, in either circumstance, research shows these young people's housing and employment prospects to be invariably poor.

Many children are, therefore, as much victims of domestic violence as their mothers. This research shows that children's reactions to living in a violent situation may often be very similar to those of children who experience other traumatic events, including such diversity as the Hillsborough stadium disaster or sexual abuse. All the available research suggests that there is no 'quick-fix' for children who have suffered in this way, and those who have grown up with domestic violence should be entitled as of right to on-going help and support, if they need it, in the same way as others who have survived a natural disaster or endured a more direct type of abuse.

Government's responsibility to reform public policy and lead a shift in popular attitudes which presently serve to underpin violent relationships

All the evidence from this study shows that living in a violent situation is profoundly damaging to mothers and their children, and yet this research also demonstrates how extremely hard it is for women to leave violent situations and how difficult professionals find it to intervene effectively to help them to do so.

In large part, these problems are intrinsic to domestic violence because of the nature of the power and control which men in violent relationships usually come to wield over their female partners and often their children. Within the intimacy of these relationships, and especially within the family home, violent men's power becomes magnified, thus explaining why most women in these situations feel genuinely terrified and sometimes quite convinced that they will never be able to escape from their violent partners. The research shows that women's feelings of being utterly trapped in an intolerable relationship are often increased by their depression, exhaustion and isolation.

However important the power and control inherent in violent relationships may be in preventing women from leaving their violent partners, it is vital to recognise that it is 'external factors' which, perhaps often unintentionally, reinforce men's power in these violent relationships. These external factors include housing and social security policy, police policy and practice and the civil and criminal law. All these external factors are central government responsibilities and susceptible to change.

Reforms in these areas could make it much easier for women to make the decision to leave and would also, therefore, alter the power relationship between them and their violent partners in their favour. For part of the hold men have over mothers and children in violent relationships lies in their shared knowledge that if the woman leaves she faces a very uncertain future in terms of housing, income and protection from him.

The question, for example, arises of why mothers and children should have physically to leave their home, with all the consequent disruption to their lives which this entails, in order to escape from the violent man. He is, after all, the one at fault, not them. This study shows that the upheaval of having to leave home is a great disincentive to mothers wishing to end a violent relationship. Yet, under present arrangements, physically quitting their home is probably the only reasonably safe 'option' for women with violent partners because of the generally poor protection afforded to them by the civil (and criminal) law. Again, a much more determined, strategic approach to deterring violent men from harassing women and children would make it much easier for women to end violent relationships.

Central government, therefore, has a crucial role to play in terms of the reform of public policy but also has a responsiblity to encourage a change in public attitudes about domestic violence. Almost all of the mothers taking part in this research said they found it difficult to decide if it was better for their children whether they stayed or left. This indecision was due in large part to concerns about poverty and housing issues for women who leave, as already discussed, but some mothers were also worried about the adverse emotional impact on their children of being without a father – albeit a violent one. Mothers need to understand that children who grow up in violent situations invariably suffer damage in the short and the long term, and that having a violent father in their children's home is much more harmful to both them and their children than not having a father at home at all.

Positive steps must be taken by central government to give clear messages to men and women that: domestic violence damages children and their mothers; domestic violence is wrong and a crime; and that the violence is always the responsibility of the perpetrator, and never of those who are the victims. If mothers and children in violent relationships could be relieved of some of the shame, embarassment and guilt they often feel, they would find it much easier to regain some control over the lives and to begin to recover from the traumatic effects of their experiences.

Recommendations

Domestic violence is known to be a widespread problem affecting families who are wealthy, poor or of average income. This survey and others reveal the guilt and shame caused by domestic violence and mothers' and children's reluctance to reveal it – even where social workers may be aware of a problem. The difficulty in finding a response lies in three areas: ensuring all agencies work together, reinforcing the complexity of the issue and underlining the needs of children.

More help for children living with domestic violence

- All children living in violent situations must be considered to be 'children in need' under the Children Act, and Government must fund local authorities so that they are able to implement these provisions of the Children Act in full.

- Local authorities must ensure that children living with domestic violence are offered appropriate support and help. A range of services are required to meet the varying needs of children of different ages:

1   Visits from social workers to offer advice, assistance and counselling as required

2   Counselling and play therapy for children who have left violent situations to enable them to overcome the trauma associated with the violence

3   Counselling for mothers so that they are better able to meet the needs of their children

4   Family mediation and supervised access arrangements for those situations in which mothers have left violent partners and it is safe and in the interests of children for them to keep in touch with their fathers

5   Multi-disciplinary support programmes for young people who have grown up in violent situations where there is concern about the effects of their experiences on their behaviour

6   Top up education programmes to help young people who have lost out on their schooling through domestic violence.

Working together to respond to domestic violence

- Local agencies (education, police, housing, social services, doctors and health visitors) must come together in Domestic Violence Fora to provide a multi-agency response to domestic violence. The needs of children living in violent situations must be at the top of the agenda at such meetings, and services must be available to meet those needs. A key task should be to focus on how the various agencies work together to identify families living with violence and ensure they are offered the help they need. A key responsibility of the Fora should be to provide an advice line for professionals working with children and families. This should provide advice on domestic violence and its impact on children and information on how to respond and get access to the help children may need.

Better support for mothers and children to help them to leave violent situations

- All mothers and children who leave violent situations must have priority access to permanent, affordable housing, without having to spend more than a very short time in temporary accommodation.

- This right should extend to mothers and children who move to a different area to escape domestic violence.

- Government must abandon its plans to amend the homelessness legislation because these mean that mothers and children would lose their right to permanent re-housing.

- Funding for women's refuges must be enhanced and put on a secure footing. Provision should be increased from one family refuge place per 30,000 population to one per 10,000 population.

- Mothers should have priority access to welfare benefits as soon as they have left a violent situation.

- Lone mothers should be offered access to affordable child care and appropriate education and training so that they are able to work to support themselves and their children.

Greater protection for mothers and children suffering violence

- The Law Commission's recommendations must be urgently implemented so that there is a presumption in favour of powers of arrest being attached to injunctions.

- Police protection for women suffering violence must be improved. Enhanced police protection, including the installation of panic buttons, should be offered to those women who have experienced severe or recurrent violence.

Better access for mothers and children to help and advice

- Government should provide for the establishment of a nationwide, 24 hour domestic violence helpline for women and children. This should be as widely publicised as *ChildLine* is today.

- Government must ensure that every local authority establishes at least one confidential, community based support service for mothers and children suffering from domestic violence. Existing family centres may be suitable places in which to base these resources.

- Government must ensure that local authorities publish a range of helpful information leaflets for mothers and children experiencing domestic violence and disseminate this widely through doctors' surgeries, schools, libraries etc. Domestic Violence Units should be reviewed and quality standards set.

Heightening the awareness of key professionals

- Police training must be improved so that all police officers, not just those in specialist units, have a better understanding of the impact of domestic violence on children. They must always carry out their overriding duty to protect children and women in violent situations.

- Training and guidance about domestic violence for the judiciary must be improved so that the courts always treat violence against women and children with the seriousness it deserves.

- Education for the key professionals who come into contact with children and mothers (e.g. teachers, social workers, doctors, health visitors) must include better information about the impact of domestic violence and guidance on the appropriate action for them to take for the protection and benefit of children. They should be empowered to alert social services to children living in violent households so that a social worker can visit and appropriate support can be offered.

- Training for professionals (including police officers, youth workers, probation officers and social workers) who encounter vulnerable young people who are at risk or in trouble must be improved so that they are aware of the possible impact of domestic violence on young people's attitudes and behaviour.

More public education about domestic violence and its effects

- A rolling public education campaign targetted at people living in violent relationships must be launched. It must stress that domestic violence has dramatic short and longer term effects on children and their mothers and that such violence is a crime and always the fault of the perpetrator, not the victims.

- The PSHE curriculum in schools should contain material stressing the unacceptability of violence in personal relationships, including some sensitive written material to help those children living with domestic violence.

- Government should reverse its recent decision to allow childminders to 'smack' children in their care.

Appendix one: supplementary tables

Table A: Mothers' experience of abuse and domestic violence

Frequency %s

Type of abuse/violence	none	once/twice	several a month
called stupid/useless	25	14	61
not given money	26	13	61
not allowed out	31	17	52
not allowed to speak to people	35	21	45
threatened with violence	12	20	68
locked in house	66	15	19
clothes taken	78	12	10
read/watch pornography	83	7	10
humiliated i.f. children	28	20	52
humiliated i.f. others	31	17	52
forced to have sex	54	27	29
slapped/punched	14	20	66
grabbed/shaken	24	21	55
kicked	39	15	46
head butted	63	14	23
strangled	37	31	32
hit by object	39	22	38
beaten i.f. children	43	18	39
sexually abused i.f. children	90	1	9
beliefs mocked	64	15	21
raped with threats	77	9	14
raped with violence	82	6	12

(107 respondents)

Table B: Injuries resulting from assaults on mothers

Frequency %s

Nature of injury	none	once/twice	several a month
bruising or black eye	17	51	31
scratches	60	16	24
broken bones	77	16	7
cuts	50	30	21

(105 respondents)

Table C: Effects of violence on mothers

Effect	%
seeing GP	43
going to hospital	40
overnight in hospital	12
had time off work	18
difficulty in sleeping	70
worried/nervous	90
depressed/no self-confidence	93

(108 respondents)

Appendix two: case studies

Case study one

'Fiona' was taken by her mother to a refuge with her brother and sisters following the disclosure from her elder sister that her father had been sexually abusing her. This was the last straw for her mother, who had experienced years of violence and abuse from her husband. Fiona was unaware of the violence which her mother had experienced – *"I never saw her crying or upset... she used to cover up the bruises... I think my sister and brother protected me a lot. They used to take me upstairs and read me stories"* – so Fiona didn't understand why they had to leave so suddenly.

Fiona didn't like being in the refuge and *"even thought about taking my Mum's pills to escape"*. After eleven weeks in the refuge, Fiona ran back to her father with her younger brother and stayed with him. *"I felt sorry for him.... when we went back he cried, said how much he missed us and that he didn't know why we had gone... He made up stories about Mum and how she didn't want us."* Fiona did not see her mother for another four years.

In fact, Fiona did not discover what had really happened in her family until she was nineteen and her father physically assaulted her. While she was recovering in hospital, Fiona's mother came to visit her and broke down and told her of the years of abuse she had suffered. *"Before that I never realised what my father was like, or what my mother had been through... I believed her... I couldn't understand why my Dad had attacked me, and she was very upset."* Fiona has since remembered witnessing several frightening incidents at home when she was a young child. *"Mum used to come into our bedroom at night and get into bed with me... I remember my father coming in and dragging her back to their bed where she belonged."*

Following her father's attack on her, Fiona sought the help of an NCH Action For Children housing and support project. This provided her not only with safe accommodation, but also gave her the chance to discuss her feelings with trained staff. One worker in particular helped Fiona to come to terms with the knowledge of the violence that had gone on in her family for all those years.

Fiona is currently living independently and has a young child of her own and is very happy. However, she is upset that she still has problematic relations with some members of her family, especially her younger brother and her father.

"(My younger brother) is just like his father..very aggressive..he has to have his own way all the time.. He's very insecure and has tried to commit suicide. I'm afraid of what my Dad might do to my daughter... but I don't want to deprive her of contact with her grandfather... I hate him."

Case study two

Sandra's husband smashed her head against the wall because her baby was making a mess while eating. He picked up the baby's dish and threw it at Sandra. She was covered in baby food. *"I collapsed on the floor."* she recalls. *"My three-year old, David, was trying to pull me across the floor. He was crying and saying, 'Mummy get up.'*

"On another occasion my husband had his hands around my throat and was dragging me round the front room. David was screaming. The baby was asleep in the cot but woke up. David was trying to pull my husband off. Eventually I sat down on the settee with the children, one on either side, and cuddled them to try and calm them down because they were both crying. Then my husband turned on me again. He punched me really hard on the leg. He tried to pull the eldest away, but he wouldn't go so I held on as tight as I could."

Sandra's experience is a depressingly typical example of domestic violence. The vicious horror of the attacks not only ruined her life and made her distrust men, it has also had a lasting effect on her children.

"I don't know if David understood what was going on at the time. He comes out with things now like. 'Oh, when I get bigger my daddy's never going to hit you again because I can look after you.' At the moment his work is suffering at school. His reading is suffering."

Eventually Sandra was able to leave her husband but it wasn't easy.

"I went to the Health Visitor and said I'd had enough. She arranged a refuge place and recommended that I left the area. But I didn't really want to, my friends were here, my family's here and my child was going to start school soon.

"Another time I tried to leave, I went to a friend with everything piled up in the buggy. He caught me and took the eldest child back. Everything happened so fast. The child was being dragged this way and that way. The police said that there was nothing they could do because he was their natural father and the child didn't seem to be in any danger. I think I proba-

bly would have left him sooner if I thought that there was no chance in hell that he was going to come and attack me."

Eventually, Sandra divorced her husband. During this time she was in contact with the Social Services Department who referred her and her children to an NCH Action For Children family centre.

"When I was introduced to the family centre I thought, 'Well I don't know it's not really my scene.'...and I've been coming here ever since. I've joined women's groups and even introduced friends to come here. I think this place is brilliant. It's somewhere you can bring the children and visit other people. My son loves it here, all the things that they can do for children are great."

Sandra's children have benefitted from the project in many ways. It is a place they enjoy coming to because of the number of toys and the space to run around. The atmosphere is joyful, friendly and caring, and this has helped them become more settled. Fear and threats no longer stalk their young lives.

Case study three

Marion is a mother of five children aged between 9 and 18. She explains how the violence of her husband has had a devastating effect, not just on her life but on the lives of her children.

"Things were all right until just after my daughter was born. Every time I picked up the baby, he would go mad... complete jealousy.One time when he was hitting me, I remember Chris and Julie (two of her children) running down the stairs with their tennis bats screaming at him, 'Leave our mummy alone!'

"They would wake up screaming and crying. At that time I thought because they are young they'll forget it...believe me it doesn't go away. It's not until adolescence when they start going through changes in themselves that all this stuff starts to come out. Julie once said to me, 'When I'm an adult, I don't want to be like you. I've seen everything that you've gone through - believe me that's not going to happen to me. I'm not going to get involved.' She's not going to get married, she daren't think about that."

Despite the persistent attacks on her, Marion found it hard to throw her husband out.

"You don't want to be told to leave him. You don't want to be told how stupid you are. You want somebody that will listen to you and maybe advise,

or talk about the children and the short and long term effects it can have. You want to be aware and wake up to what's going on, not somebody that's going to sit there and judge."

However, finally, her husband went too far.

"I was sitting cuddling Julie, I was too frightened to let him hold her, and he started ranting and raving. He got his roll up cigarette and put it on Julie's neck, and she was just a baby! So I got up, walked out the front door and left him."

Yet, leaving her husband brought about a whole new set of problems for Marion and one of her daughters, Debbie.

"If I went anywhere she was holding onto my leg. She was stuck to me. It got to the point that she wouldn't even go out of the door. Do you know what she was frightened of? She thought that she'd come home from nursery one day and I wouldn't be there. She said, 'You're going to leave me like Daddy left me'. I referred myself to a local NCH Action For Children family centre by calling Parentline. They gave me a wonderful social worker... she's been really helpful... I have said to her she is more than welcome to talk to us all, all the children, at any time, because I just feel that what's needed here is a lot of healing."

The family centre workers helped Marion's younger children realize not all men were violent, and helped to show them that men could be loving and caring. They also offered counselling to the older children.

But for Marion the slow, healing process has begun with a painful realization.

"I think the attacks have left me less loving, definitely, as a person, even towards my own children. I'm a harder person... I'm not a person for cuddles now, because it has destroyed the best side of me and I can never find that again."

Appendix three: references

1 *National inter-agency working party report on domestic violence*, Victim Support, 1992; Eekelaar and Katz, *Family violence: an international, interdisciplinary study*, Butterworths, 1978.

2 Russel, *Taking stock: refuge provisions in London in the late 1980s*, Southwark Council 1989; Eekelaar and Katz, supra.

3 Smith, *Domestic violence: an overview of the literature*, Home Office research study no. 107, 1989.

4 Dobash and Dobash, *Violence against wives*, Open Books, 1980.

5 Metropolitan Police service statistics.

6 Dobash and Dobash, supra.

7 From 770 in 1985 to 9,800 in 1992. Metropolitan Police statistics.

8 Marsden and Owens *Jekyll and Hyde marriages* in New Society, 8/5/1975.

9 Borkowski et al, *Marital violence: the community response*. Tavistock Books, 1983.

10 Straus et al, *Behind closed doors: violence in the American family* 1980; Schulman, *A survey of spousal violence against women in Kentucky*, US Department of Justice, 1979.

11 Pizzey and Shapiro, *Choosing a violent relationship* in *New Society*, 23/12/1981; *Prone to Violence*, Hamlyn, 1982.

12 Andrews, *Violence in normal families*, paper presented at the Marriage Research Centre conference, London, April 1987; Walker, *The Battered Woman*, 1979; *Psychological impact of the criminalization of domestic violence on victims*, Victimology, 10, 1985.

13 For example, Dobash and Dobash, supra.

14 For example, Wilson, *What is to be done about violence against women*, Penguin, 1983.

15 Pahl, *Private Violence and Public Policy*, RKP, 1985.

16 For example, Dobash and Dobash supra, and Roy, *Battered Women*, Van Nostrand Reinhold, 1977.

17 Evason, *Hidden violence*, Farset Press, 1982; and Klein, *Battered women and the dominance of women*, in *Judge, lawyer, victim, thief: women, gender roles and criminal justice*, Northeastern University Press, 1982.

18 Kaufman, Kantor and Straus, *The drunken bum theory of wife beating*, Social Problems, 34, 1987.

19 See for example, Rosenbaum and O'Leary, *The unintended victims of marital violence*, in the *American Journal of Orthopsychiatry* vol.51, 1981.

20 Dobash and Dobash, 1984.

21 Hilton, *Battered women's concerns about their children witnessing wife assault*, in *Journal of interpersonal violence*, vol.

7. 1992.

22   Jaffe et al, *Similarities in behavioural and social maladjustment among child victims and witnesses to family violence, American Journal of Orthopsychiatry* 1986; Wolfe et al, *Children of battered women: the relation of child behaviour to family violence and maternal stress, Journal of Consultative Clinical Psychology*, 1985.

23   Forsstrom-Cohen and Rosenbaum, *The effects of parental marital violence on young adults: an explanatory investigation*, in the *Journal of Marriage and the Family*, vol. 47, 1985.

24   Hilberman and Munson, *Sixty battered women*, in *Victimology International Journal*, vol. 2, 1977.

25   Fantuzzo and Lindquist, *The effects of observing conjugal violence on children: a review and analysis of research methodology*, in *Journal of Family Violence*, vol. 4, 1989.

26   Wolfe et al, *Children's adjustments to family violence*, in *Family abuse and its consequences: new directions in research*, edited by Hotaling, Finkelhor, Kirkpatrick and Straus, Sage 1988.

27   Straus, Gelles and Steinmetz, *Behind closed doors: violence in the American family*, Doubleday Press 1980.

28   Bowker et al, *On the relationship between wife beating and child abuse*, in *Feminist perspectives on wife abuse* edited by Bograd et al, Sage, 1988.

29   Hughes et al, *Witnessing spouse abuse and experiencing physical abuse: a double whammy?* in *Journal of family violence*, vol. 1, 1992.

30   Stockley et al, *Young people on the move*, Dept. of Psychology, University of Surrey 1993.

31   Lawrance, *The link between domestic violence and child abuse - the police response in West Yorkshire*, in *Child Abuse Review*, vol.4 1990.

32   See for example, para. 2.23 *Domestic Violence, the report of a national inter-agency working party, Victim Support*, 1992.

33   Figure quoted by Earl Russell in the House of Lords, on 29th April 1994 (Hansard 433-434).

34   The Law Commission, *Family law, domestic violence and occupation of the family home* (report no. 207), 1992, HMSO.

35   The balance of harm test would place a court under a duty to make an order if it seemed likely that the applicant or any relevant child would suffer significant harm if an order was not made, and such harm would be greater than the harm which the respondent or any relevant child would suffer is the order was made. The Law Commission recommended against introducing the principle of the welfare of the child being paramount, because of concern that this would give too little weight to the applicant's need for personal protection and might encourage more mothers to use 'I've got the